Seasons in a Country Kitchen Cookbook

SEASONS IN A
Country Kitchen
COOKBOOK

Darlene Kronschnabel

JONES
BOOKS
Madison, Wisconsin

Jones Books
309 N. Hillside Terrace
Madison, Wisconsin 53705
www.jonesbooks.com

First edition, first printing

Library of Congress Cataloging-in-Publication Data

Kronschnabel, Darlene.
    Seasons in a country kitchen cookbook / Darlene Kronschnabel.—1st ed.
        p. cm.
    Includes index.
    ISBN 0-9763539-2-X (alk. paper)
    1. Cookery, American. I. Title.
    TX715.K89885 2005
    641.5973—dc22

                                                 2005023369

Printed in the U.S.A.

To Mother and Grandmother, who not only taught me to love food and its preparation, but to deeply appreciate seasons in a country kitchen.

Table of Contents

AUTUMN

WINTER

Acknowledgments

Use of the following materials is gratefully acknowledged:

"Moving Day—Farm Style": *Green Bay Register*, March 21, 1969. Reprinted by permission of Tom Staley, Editor, *The Compass*.

"Stalking the Wild Asparagus": *Ocooch Mountain News*, May 1979. Reprinted by permission of J. D. Belanger, Publisher.

Portions of "Stalking the Wild Asparagus" and "Feeding the Threshers," appeared in *Farm Wife News*. Reprinted by permission of *Farm Wife News*, currently *Country Woman Magazine*.

"Feeding the Threshers": *Ocooch Mountain News*, Summer 1980. Reprinted by permission of J. D. Belanger, Publisher.

Portions of "Rifles and Pancakes" appeared in *Inland Steel*, March 1973. Reprinted by permission of Gwendolyn Syke, Advertising Representative, *Inland Steel*.

It is my pleasure to include poems by my mother's sister, Anne M. Diley, a Wisconsin poet, in *Seasons in a Country Kitchen Cookbook*. I would like to express my appreciation to her family for allowing Anne's work to appear in this book.

"Spring Showing," "Along a Country Road," "Neighbors," and "Grandmother," by Anne M. Diley, as appeared in *Walking Down a Country Road*, Royal One Publishing, Research Triangle Park, NC 27709-2017. Reprint permission granted by Paula Diley, Author/Editor, January 8, 2005.

Introduction

A Seasonal Treasury of Country Kitchen Recipes and Fond Memories

In these days of eating out, carrying out, food fads, junk food, quick service, and all-around hurry, hurry, we can get quite nostalgic for times when life's pace was slower and quieter. So I invite you to come along with me.

Together, under blue skies, we'll meander down a country road lined with purple clover and golden black-eyed Susans. The meadowlark's song and the scent of new-mown hay drifts through the air. It's a gentle curving road, this country road. It's a road I travel quite often. It's the one that leads me back to the country kitchens of my childhood.

For me, it was an exciting world, filled with Fourth of July family reunions, potluck neighborhood parties, harvest crew dinners, and country-style holiday celebrations. I fondly recall the warm conversations and hearty laughter shared with family and friends.

And, of course, I remember the food. We savored the brimming bowls of garden-fresh peas and tiny new potatoes, parsley coated and lightly kissed with melted butter and hot milk. No one ever passed up Mother's large platters of chicken and dumplings or her buttermilk biscuits and gravy. In fact, they reached for second and third helpings. The simplest desserts often included warm hickory nut cinnamon rolls, wild blackberry cobbler topped with whipped cream, and pie made from just-picked wild blueberries. Even a modest slice of her warm homemade bread slathered with spicy apple butter drew raves.

These are just a few of the familiar dishes we now call comfort foods. Dishes such as these trigger memories of yesterday's country kitchens, where delectable aromas filled the air. Everything tasted better back then. Of course, those were the days before commercial fertilizers and pest-controlling chemicals.

Wild and garden-ripened produce came to the table fresh and full-flavored. Still, the warmth generated by these memories does help improve the flavor of our comfort foods.

With a dash of nostalgia, a scoop of country kitchen lore, a sprinkle of laughter, and more than 200 old-fashioned home-style recipes, *Seasons in a Country Kitchen Cookbook* takes you on a journey down memory lane with me. Together we'll step into the traditional farm kitchen of yesterday. Along the way there's a collection of made-from-scratch recipes and country kitchen stories I've gathered.

I come by my love of country cooking naturally, as my Hungarian grandmother and mother shared a lifelong interest in it. In visiting their kitchen, you soon realized a good deal of their time was spent thinking and talking about food and various ways of cooking. Their friends and neighbors were no different. A time-honored tradition among these country cooks was, and still is, recipe swapping.

My enjoyment of country life and its cooking style led my husband and me into the farm vacation business. The guests who came to our Ridgeside Farm in Waukesha County not only enjoyed the homemade country cooking, but ended their stay with requests for my recipes.

The interest and encouragement of my guests led me to begin writing my "Recipes from a Country Kitchen" column that ran for ten years in Wisconsin, Illinois, and Minnesota newspapers. Another column, "From My Country Kitchen," appeared in a national publication. Nine cookbooks followed. Many of them focused on the style and tastes I enjoyed long ago in my mother's farm kitchen.

Seasons in a Country Kitchen Cookbook is an invitation to journey back to a long-ago country kitchen to sample the cooking and memories. Here is a cuisine based on seasonal farm-fresh produce and family approval. The handed-down recipes have been updated to reflect today's cooking methods, but all have remained as unpretentious, honest, and heartwarming as the farm families that enjoyed them. It's a way to share with you the pleasures of old-fashioned cooking dished up with warmth and hospitality to be enjoyed casually and comfortably—the true country style.

My Mother's Country Kitchen

Looking back, it seems as if my mother's country kitchen was always filled with a fascinating combination of events, people, and foods. There, I acquired knowledge and the traditions that have remained basically the same throughout my life. I now realize I did not acquire these treasured gifts in a single country kitchen. It took a number of them. We lived in several rural Wisconsin communities when I was growing up. My father, a hard-working tenant farmer like others in the late-Depression years, kept seeking land to call his own. In later years, he finally realized his dream of owning a farm.

As often as we moved, both parents encouraged us to look on the bright side. Moving gave us an opportunity to meet and enjoy new neighbors, who in turn became dear friends. Each neighborhood had its own ethnic groups of German, Polish, Irish, and Dutch farmers. For nearly all of them, their communities and cultures had changed little since their northern European ancestors settled in Wisconsin.

An independent and self-sufficient man, my father determined that no matter how many times we moved, our lives continued as always, secure and happy in the family circle. Together, my parents made sure that beyond the daily farm chores, laughter, and warmth flourished in our country kitchen. My brothers and I clearly grasped the values of honesty, responsibility, and character strength along with the value of a job well done.

Money, of course was in short supply. It provided only the bare necessities of food and clothing. I suppose by today's standards, we were poor. Our homes weren't "modern" and we had very few luxuries. It seems strange now, but as a child I never noticed that. It was something we didn't talk about. Instead, my father focused on the positive.

"There's no reason for farm folks to go hungry," he'd often say after the meal's blessing. "A full wood shed and a garden well tended is all you need to keep from going to bed cold and hungry." And he was right.

Firewood, for both cooking and heating, came from the farm woodlots. The farm animals supplied us with beef, pork, and veal. The dairy herd gave us all the milk we needed for drinking and cooking. Mother always raised a flock of chickens and a few ducks. Each year she planted a large vegetable garden that included rhubarb and strawberry plants along with raspberry and currant bushes. Back then, apple and plum orchards were common on most farms. Sometimes we even found cherry trees.

What Mother didn't grow in the garden, we found growing wild. Hickory and choke cherry trees along with hazelnut and gooseberry bushes grew in the woodlots and along fence lines. So did blackberries, blueberries, dewberries, and raspberries. Wild asparagus flourished along fences bordering gravel roads. Once, to Mother's delight, we found a patch of caraway plants growing in a roadside ditch. Wild game, both four-legged and feathered, was plentiful. So were the fish from nearby streams, rivers, and lakes. We ate what was ripe and fresh at the moment. What we didn't consume in season, Mother canned or froze.

We were country people with simple tastes. We just happened to have a resident Hungarian grandmother in our country kitchen. That made all the difference in the world.

My grandparents came to this country in the early 1900s from Budapest, and they brought their tastes and recipes with them. When my grandfather passed away, Grandma Wezmarovich came to live with us. My memories of her are bound up in countless family gatherings in our country kitchen and the lingering aroma of goulash slowly simmering on the old wood range. Her distinctive coffee cakes—made with nuts, poppy seeds, and butter, which gave them an irresistible fragrance—were always eaten warm. They never lasted long enough to grow cold.

Her usual method of measuring consisted of handfuls, pinches, dashes, sprinkles, and, as she put it, "going by the tongue and the eye." Grandma Wezmarovich took the simple and inexpensive things and added heaping spoons of paprika, two or three onions, as many—if not more— large cloves of garlic, a scoop of sour cream, and, yes, the poppy seeds. Not all at once, mind you. She was, after all, a very selective cook. That was why the dishes she brought to the table tasted like ambrosia.

In the 1930s and early '40s, in the days before rural electrification and modern machinery, country life was, as it is now, serious business and hard work. Outside, the men went about their daily chores of tending the cattle and milking two times a day. As sure as planting followed spring tilling, threshing followed haying. The summer sun and rain nurtured the growing corn from golden kernels to tall stalks until it eventually ripened for picking and silo filling. Fall plowing, in a race to beat the winter snow, followed the final harvesting. At times, it seemed as if cutting and sawing firewood for heating and cooking took all winter. The seasons, in their fashion, wrapped around us and sped by. The sunup-to-sundown chores and fieldwork created demanding appetites.

Inside, this meant three meals a day, 365 days a year, needed to be prepared and ready to be served. Lots of hard work and loving care went into those meals. For as long as I can remember, being in the middle of Mother's country kitchen was the most exciting place to be. I spent many happy hours keeping a watchful eye on all the fascinating rituals. I enjoyed the nose-twitching aroma of warm bread fresh from the oven and homemade yeast doughnuts dipped in sugar and cinnamon. Nowhere else could I savor the heady scent of cooking cabbage rolls or paprika chicken, hot apple pie or spicy soft molasses cookies. Best of all, beyond watching, I got to sample and experiment.

Mother baked eight loaves of bread, all kneaded by hand, every Tuesday, Thursday, and Saturday. I helped by buttering the pans and punching down the rising dough. As I grew older, she taught me how to shape the loaves and how to tell when they were ready for the wood stove's hot oven. The baking aroma alone was enough to make my mouth water, but to see the exquisite golden loaves was too tempting. One bite of a thick slice of warm bread slathered with butter and a cold glass of milk and I was in heaven.

While my mother enjoyed cooking and took pride in the meals she prepared, she loved the outdoors and gardening. Under her wing, I learned how to scatter wood ashes on cucumber vines to discourage bugs; how to tell when the garden peas were ready for picking; to let the sun dry the dew from the yellow beans before disturbing the bushes. I learned how to snatch an egg from under a broody hen's clutch—and how to tell the difference between a fresh egg and one scheduled for hatching.

In the kitchen, she wasted no time in introducing me to the wonders of country cooking. At age eight, I was baking cakes and cookies for the family. Encouraged, I moved on to master the simple things such as meatloaf and vegetable cooking. She taught me that blue enamel pans were a must for turning out succulent roasts and showed me the value of cast-iron frying skillets as well as how to humor the big Monarch wood-burning range. By the time I reached fourteen, I was comfortable preparing family meals that often included roast beef, potatoes and gravy, coleslaw, buttered carrots, and chocolate cake with white frosting. The praises my father repeated while eating the meals I cooked and served were music to my ears. It was all the encouragement I needed to follow in my mother's and grandmother's footsteps.

On the farm, the noon meal is called dinner and the evening meal is called supper. Because of the farm routine, breakfast and dinner were very large meals. Supper, served in late afternoon before the evening milking, was generally lighter fare. Most often, it consisted of fried potatoes and leftovers from dinner.

While I was growing up, there never seemed to be just family around the dinner table. There were the hired men, harvest crews, drop-in neighbors, city relatives, and an assortment of itinerant peddlers that ranged from the Watkins, McNess, and Raleigh salesmen to cattle buyers, horse traders, and scrap iron and rag men. Dad took it for granted, and mother agreed, anyone visiting the farm at midday was automatically invited in for dinner. Food, they believed, was a thing to be shared.

I remember my mother pausing in the middle of a hectic day to tell me, "We make do with what we have. It isn't a question of how to make it look good, but making sure there is enough to offer strangers should they drop in." True to her lifelong philosophy, there was always plenty to go around no matter how many unexpected guests pulled a chair up to her dinner table.

My father enjoyed company and after-dinner conversation. "What's your hurry?" he'd asked anyone about to leave. "Sit a bit and let your meal settle."

These were the times I enjoyed most. I listened in awe to stories of northern Wisconsin's logging days, barn raisings, runaway horses, farm accidents, harvesting and weather related joys and woes, past and present auction prices, hunting and fishing tales combined with local news.

As my father listened with good humor, he cautioned me, "You need to take some of those tales with a grain of salt." I just laughed and told him I'd already figured that out.

As the years passed, I left home to work, eventually married, settled into a country kitchen of my own and began my writing career. It was only then that I fully realized my good fortune of growing up on a Wisconsin farm with the loving guidance of a mother who just happened to be a terrific Hungarian cook. Last, but perhaps the most important of all, I married a man who appreciates the many blessings of country kitchen traditions and the cooking that comes with it.

The years have moved along so quickly. Grandma and my parents are gone now and I miss them dearly. My memory clings to the exciting days on those long-ago farms and the happy times I spent in my mother's country kitchen.

Today, as I thumb through her dog-eared and smudged recipe files, I can see her in my mind's eye. She's standing at the old Monarch range, stirring a kettle of bubbling chili or maybe she's slicing boiled potatoes into her favorite cast-iron skillet. She's wearing a floral feed sack apron over her cotton housedress, telling me how her mother would stress, "If you want people to enjoy the food you cook, you have to enjoy cooking it."

As I ruffle her time-worn recipe cards in my hand, I understand that by simply preparing these wonderful dishes, I can get the feeling I'm back again in Mother's country kitchen. But most important of all, I realize that her special brand of kitchen wisdom still gladdens my heart.

A Note to the Reader

Don't for a minute believe that all of yesterday's country cooking was a series of complicated recipes. Farm wives didn't have time for fancy cooking in their everyday meals. And since cooking for hearty appetites was a big responsibility, you know that the favorite stand-by recipes used by our grandmothers and mothers had to be good.

They planted, cultivated, and harvested ripe vegetables and fruits from their gardens. What they didn't grow, they picked wild. Farm-raised animals provided all the fresh meat a family needed.

Not everyone today has the opportunity to pamper a garden or enjoy the seasonal abundance our grandmothers and mothers had. However, we do have roadside stands and farmers' markets offering, from late spring to late fall, an irresistible assortment of fresh produce. Here you'll get a chance to meet and visit with the growers, ask them questions, and receive personalized answers on how to cook, serve, and store their produce. The popularity of these markets proves that fresh, from-scratch country cooking is still respected and enjoyed.

Yes, the recipes our grandmothers and mothers used called for butter, lard, bacon fat, cream, sour cream, and eggs. Even the sugar in some of these recipes seems excessive. While we may be health-conscious today, yesterday's hard-working farm cooks never considered these products a hazard; they were using the ingredients on hand.

Farm families used raw milk for drinking and cooking. Ours was no exception. Considering that my father had a mixed herd of Guernsey, Brown Swiss, and Holstein milk cows, the butterfat content of our "house milk" was far higher than even that of whole milk on supermarket shelves today. The closest you can come to its full flavor is by mixing store brand whole milk with half and half.

If you have concerns with any of these calorie-rich and cholesterol-laden ingredients, simply check out the vast array of margarine, butter-flavored vegetable shortenings, and salad oils, lite and fat-free products on your supermarket shelves for substitutions. Grandma herself may have used them if they'd been available in her day. Experiment, modify, and adjust the recipe to meet your family's needs and tastes. A little tinkering on a recipe is not going to change it that much. Goodness knows Grandma did it all the time.

Measuring spoons? Measuring cups? Not many cooks used them in yesterday's country kitchens. A dab, a pinch, or a sprinkle worked just fine. So did Dad's coffee cup. Let me encourage you to use the same method, if it fits your cooking style. As you gain confidence, you'll learn to trust your instincts on how a teaspoon of salt looks in the palm of your hand; how a dash of hot sauce or chili powder spices up your soup and casseroles or how a sprinkle of ground nutmeg makes an apple pie special.

After all, "season to taste" is as important today as it was in yesterday's home-style country cooking.

S P R I N G

Spring Showing

Elf artists are mixing their colors,
The best of their golds and their blues,
With rollicking reds for the roses,
And lavender hyacinth hues.

A pretty pink rose they'll paint here,
A gay yellow daffodil there,
Touch tulips with multiple colors
As they dance away on the air.

Elf artists are mixing their colors
And trying them out one by one,
With splashes of green on the meadow,
Bright blue as a frame for the sun.

They'll mix and they'll match 'til they're perfect
And they'll put them all on display
When they pull back the curtains of springtime
And give us a morning in May.

Anne M. Diley (1916–1969)

Moving Day—Farm Style

Recipes in This Chapter

Country wisdom decreed the first weeks of March as moving time on the farm. To the best of my knowledge this wasn't a written rule. It simply made sense. Or so my father claimed. According to him, the land was still too wet for working so we'd have time to settle in before we'd need to start planting. Plus, it was only a couple of months until pasture, so there wasn't much cattle feed to move.

Those who have never experienced a move from one farm to another have no idea of the camaraderie of country neighbors, the closeness of those willing to lend a helping hand, both inside and out. Moving farm machinery, cattle, their straw bedding, and feed along with our household goods was no easy task and didn't happen in a single day. It called for a lot of helping hands from neighbors, especially those with strong young sons. Once the word went out that we were moving, my father had all the volunteer help he needed. Neighborhoods were like that back in the 1940s and '50s. Besides, there wasn't much else going on in early March.

I remember parts of many moves. Each had their exciting moments, but generally they all fit into a pattern.

It never seemed to fail that on the days Dad picked to move, the skies either threatened snow or a full-blown howling blizzard greeted us at dawn. Drifting snow and sub-zero temperatures lingered in the following days despite blue skies and bright sunshine.

The moving crew faced one challenge after another starting with snow banks, slippery roads, frozen pipes, and a wood stove heater that was too hot to handle. During one move, after a long, cold day of last-minute packing in a drafty house, the truck loaded with all our household goods slid off the icy road on a steep hill. Later, that same day, a truck tire went flat just short of the driveway to the new house.

Mother and Grandma started packing in the basement weeks in advance. They hand-wrapped each Mason jar of canned fruit or vegetables in newspaper and packed them in bushel baskets.

"Be careful not to overload the baskets," Dad warned. "You don't want bottoms giving out halfway up the basement steps."

Mother merely nodded. She hadn't put in hours filling the jars during the hot summer in a steaming kitchen to have that happen.

The two women emptied the sauerkraut crock, sacked the potatoes, carrots, parsnips, rutabagas, and turnips. Then they moved on to packing dishes in barrels and baskets upstairs. Finally, Mother took the curtains down, washed and laid them aside for the new house. All this time Dad hauled feed and machinery to the new place.

Mother woke us early on moving day.

"Hurry, eat your breakfast," she prodded. "As soon as you're done let the fire go out." Letting the fire die in the black kitchen range and in the large Round Oak heaters was always a problem for her. She had trouble deciding if she wanted a warm house in which to finish packing or a warm one waiting for her.

"Save the ashes," Mother told us, "set them on the porch so the men have them for under the wheels if the truck gets stuck."

"Hurry, wash the dishes so we're finished packing when the men come to load," she went on.

"Hurry, make some sandwiches."

"Hurry, fold the blankets and get the beds ready to knock down."

"Hurry, dress the little ones and take them to the neighbors so they don't catch cold in this drafty house."

"Hurry. . . . Hurry. . . . Hurry."

So she rushed from room to room finishing last-minute packing before the men arrived.

Most times Dad arranged with our milk hauler to move the household belongings. There was one drawback to this system. The milk truck always came late in the morning, as the driver needed to finish his route to the local cheese factory. No one used dollies in those days to move the cumbersome stoves and sofas. The men simply put their shoulders to the heavy cast-iron stove, grunting and groaning, until finally jostling it into place on the truck.

After what seemed like hours, the open milk truck was loaded and the tailgate locked in place. Kitchen chairs rested upside down on the dining room buffet. Cartons and baskets of dishes and earthen crocks filled the space under the table legs. Bed headboards, springs, and mattresses bucked the wind at the front of the load. As the truck rounded the corner, a dresser drawer slid out and its contents ruffled in the wind.

Down the road the driver pulled into a neighbor's driveway. "Got orders to stop for a bite to eat," he answered Mother's questioning look.

Inside, we discovered a feast to equal a thresher's meal. Marie, Vi, and Myrtle and several other of Mother's friends scurried around placing hot platters of sliced roast beef and meat loaf on the table. A trio of steaming casseroles that included scalloped potatoes and ham, beef and cabbage, and pork noodle hot dish followed. And there were bowls of pickles, beets, apples, and both sweet and sour cucumber scattered about the table.

The table looked full to me, but they continued to find room for dishes of coleslaw, fruit-filled gelatin, buttered peas and carrots, and creamed green beans. Plates of homemade bread, double stacked, fit in on each end of the table. I even saw platters of my favorite chocolate chip date and cherry cakes waiting on the side table.

"Come in. Find a place and help yourself," the women waved us forward. "The first shift has already eaten, but there's still plenty for everyone."

The warm room alone was a welcome relief after the bone-chilling cold of the rapidly emptying old house. However, it was the heavenly aroma drifting from the food-laden table that was almost more than my ten-year-old system could tolerate. My mother stood silently in the doorway staring at the spread of food on her neighbor's dining room table.

Marie walked over and put her arms around Mother's shoulders. "Now don't you go tearing up on us," she said. "You certainly didn't think your neighbors would let you go without a hot meal, did you?"

"I guess I was too busy to think," Mother admitted.

With a loaded truck waiting for them, the moving crew didn't linger long at the table. Before I had a chance at a second piece of cake, they were heading out the door.

My brothers and I tumbled over each other in our rush into the new house. Of course Mother and Dad had seen it before, but we had to wait until moving day to have our first look. We ran from room to room checking the layout and seeking the best area to claim as our own. I can still see the eerie shadows cast on unfamiliar walls and feel the shivers that ran up my spine when I peeked into dark corners. Most of all, I remember my grandmother finding her rocking chair and holding the baby close so he wouldn't mind the newness.

Dinner over and cleared, the ladies from the old neighborhood arrived to help Mother settle in her new home. They scrubbed the floors, the cupboards in the pantry and put fresh paper on the shelves. They washed and dried dishes. The pots and pans found their way to a new spot. Granted, it took Mother awhile to get used to the new arrangement, but that was part of every move.

No matter how my mother tried to direct traffic, some boxes marked for the kitchen ended up in the attic. She once even found the basement baskets of empty fruit jars hiding in a second-floor bedroom closet.

Outside, Dad had his problems, too, as he helped the men unload the cattle. Wells always froze up on moving day and stanchion parts were missing. As if those things weren't enough, frightened animals fought the move by running in every direction but the right one. Men yelled and prodded. Finally, the last load of cows came in.

Dad always said the hardest part of any move was the first chore time in the new barn. Strange stalls, strange milking time, and strange feed made the animals hard to handle.

Once he grabbed what he thought was a gunnysack of chickens and dumped it in the hen house. Instead it was the sack of barn cats some young helper misplaced. Wild and with their backs arched and bristling, the clawing cats sent the chickens into a sudden molt. When the feathers and fur settled, the men stood in helpless laughter at the hissing cats in one corner and the squawking hens in another. Things like this helped to lighten the load of a hard day.

During some of our moves, I remember whole families coming to welcome us to the new neighborhood. Sometimes they brought a kettle of hot chili or a cake. One welcome I will never forget happened about chore time on moving day. A car pulled into the yard just as Dad came out of the kitchen door. An elderly man rolled down the car window and called out.

"Hey, do you folks play cards?"

"Sure do," Dad answered.

"Good, we'll be over to see you when the curtains are up."

The settling in began.

Country Meat Loaf

If there's any meat dish in a farm kitchen that has more variations, I haven't found it. Every country cook I know has their favorite meat loaf recipe. It's likely she makes it the way her mother did, who made it the way grandmother did, who made it the way great-grandmother did. This popular and faithful staple can be served plain or as fancy as you like. Best of all, cold meat loaf makes a terrific sandwich.

Nonstick spray coating
2 slightly beaten eggs
1 cup milk
1 cup soft whole wheat bread crumbs
3/4 cup finely diced onion
1/2 cup finely diced celery
1/4 cup snipped parsley

1 teaspoon salt
1/4 teaspoon pepper
1/4 teaspoon ground sage
1/4 teaspoon ground thyme
1 pound lean ground beef
1/2 pound bulk pork sausage
1/3 cup catsup

Preheat oven to 350°. Lightly spray a 9 x 5 x 2-inch baking pan with nonstick spray coating. In a mixing bowl, combine eggs and milk. Stir in bread crumbs, onions, celery, parsley, salt, pepper, sage, and thyme. Add beef and pork, breaking the meat apart. Thoroughly blend meat and seasonings. Mix lightly; too much handing will produce a meat loaf with a compact texture. Mixing with your hands can be easier than with a spoon. Spoon meat mixture into prepared pan. Level the top and brush with catsup. Bake for about 1 hour or until cooked through and top is nicely browned. Allow to cool for about 15 minutes. To serve, cut into 1/2-inch slices. Makes about 8 to 10 servings.

NOTE: You can vary this basic recipe by replacing the pork sausage with either ground pork or with 1/4 pound ground pork and 1/4 pound ground veal. In place of milk, use tomato juice, catsup, or diluted canned soups. Fresh or cooked vegetables add texture and flavor. Rolled, crushed crackers or cornflakes—even seasoned stuffing mix—can be used in place of bread crumbs. You also can use different herbs and seasoning for flavoring.

Savory Pork Casserole

A family favorite and best of all, it carries well and tastes great.

2 tablespoons shortening
1 1/2 pounds pork shoulder, cut into
    bite-sized pieces
3/4 cup water
1 cup chopped onions
1 cup chopped celery
1 clove garlic, minced
1/2 teaspoon ground thyme

2 teaspoons salt, divided
3 cups uncooked broad egg noodles
1/4 teaspoon pepper
1 can cream of mushroom soup
2 cups cooked peas
2 tablespoons diced pimiento
1 cup shredded cheddar cheese
1 cup buttered bread crumbs*

In a large skillet, melt shortening over medium-high heat. Add pork and cook until thoroughly browned. Add water, onions, celery, garlic, thyme, and 1 teaspoon salt. Lower heat. Cook covered until meat is tender, about 1 hour. Meanwhile, grease a large ovenproof casserole. Preheat oven to 375°. Cook noodles according to package directions. Drain. Combine with pork mixture. Add pepper and remaining salt. Blend in mushroom soup, peas, and pimiento. Turn into prepared casserole. Top with cheese and then bread crumbs. Bake for 30 minutes or until thoroughly heated. Makes 8 to 10 servings.

*Buttered Bread Crumbs

Spread soft butter over day-old bread. Pull bread into crumbs with fork or use fingers to tear it into small pieces.

Scalloped Potatoes with Ham and Cheese

As a rule, country cooks never needed a recipe for scalloped potatoes. Mother simply peeled one potato for each person she expected for dinner, then she added two more. After slicing each potato about 1/2 inch thick she layered them in a buttered casserole. Next she sprinkled several tablespoons of flour over the potatoes, added salt and pepper, dotted them with butter, and poured milk over the mixture. The potatoes went into a hot oven to bake for about an hour. This made a tasty side dish.

However, when she wanted to serve scalloped potatoes for a special occasion or to take to a potluck dinner, she added several extra ingredients such as onions, ham, and cheese. They transformed her plain scalloped potatoes into a special main dish.

1/3 cup butter
1/3 cup all-purpose flour
1 teaspoon salt
1/4 teaspoon pepper
4 cups milk
8 cups thinly sliced potatoes (about
    6–8 medium potatoes)

3 cups fully cooked cubed ham
1 1/2 cups shredded cheddar cheese
1 cup chopped onions
1 tablespoon snipped parsley
1 teaspoon paprika

Preheat oven to 375°. Butter a 3-quart ovenproof casserole. In a medium saucepan over medium heat, melt butter. Blend in flour, salt, and pepper. Add milk gradually. Cook until thickened and smooth, stirring constantly. Set white sauce aside. Layer half the potatoes in prepared casserole. Add half the ham, cheese, and onions. Repeat the layers, ending with the cheese. Pour white sauce over potato mixture. Make sure all the potatoes are coated. Sprinkle with parsley and paprika. Bake, uncovered, for about 1 hour or until potatoes are tender and the top is evenly browned. Makes about 8 to 10 servings.

NOTE: You can substitute 1/4 pound of dried beef for the ham.

Calico Salad

This is a colorful make-ahead salad.

2 cups cooked green beans
2 cups cooked sliced carrots
2 cups cooked whole kernel corn
2 tablespoons chopped onions
Celery seed dressing*

In a large mixing bowl, combine beans, carrots, corn, and onions. Toss with celery seed dressing. Chill in covered container several hours or overnight. Serve cold. Makes about 4 to 6 servings.

*Celery Seed Dressing

1/2 cup packed brown sugar
1/3 cup cider vinegar
2 teaspoons salt
2 teaspoons celery seed
1/8 teaspoon ground mustard
Dash pepper

In a small bowl, combine sugar, vinegar, salt, celery seed, and mustard. Beat to mix well. Serve on calico salad. Makes about 3/4 cup.

Nutty Coleslaw

This is a crisp and crunchy salad.

2 1/2 cups shredded cabbage
1/2 cup chopped celery
1/4 cup diced green pepper
1/4 cup diced cucumber
1/4 cup diced onion
1/4 teaspoon salt

Dash of pepper
1/2 cup toasted walnuts*
1/2 cup mayonnaise
2 tablespoons milk
Paprika for garnish, optional

In a large mixing bowl, combine cabbage, celery, green pepper, cucumber, and onion. Mix well. Stir in salt and pepper. Just before serving add walnuts. In a small bowl, blend together mayonnaise and milk; blend well into cabbage mixture. Garnish with a sprinkle of paprika, if desired. Makes about 3 to 4 servings.

*Toasting Walnuts

Spread walnuts in a thin layer on a shallow baking pan. Bake in a 350° oven, stirring once or twice, for 5 to 10 minutes or until light golden brown.

Featherbeds (Pan Rolls)

Mashed potatoes add extra lightness and flavor to these rolls.

Water
2 large potatoes, peeled and
    quartered
1/3 cup sugar
1 teaspoon salt
1/4 cup butter or margarine
3/4 cup hot potato water, or hot
    water

1/4 cup warm water
1 package active dry yeast
1 beaten egg
1/2 cup lukewarm mashed potatoes
4 1/2 cups all-purpose flour, or as
    needed, divided
Melted butter, as needed

In a medium saucepan cook potatoes in water to cover until tender. Drain,
reserving potato water. Mash potatoes. Lightly grease a large bowl. In a small
bowl, stir sugar, salt, and butter into hot potato water. Cool to lukewarm. In a
large mixing bowl, add warm water and sprinkle in yeast, stirring until
dissolved. Add lukewarm potato water mixture, egg, mashed potatoes, and 2
cups flour to yeast. Beat until smooth. Stir in enough additional flour to form
soft dough. Turn out onto lightly floured board and knead until smooth and
elastic for about 8 to 10 minutes. Place dough in prepared bowl, turning to
grease top. Cover. Let rise in warm place, free from drafts, for about 1 hour or
until doubled. Meanwhile, grease two 9-inch round baking pans. Punch dough
down. Turn out onto lightly floured board and divide in half. To shape pan
rolls: Divide 1/2 of dough into 12 equal parts. Form into smooth balls. Place in
prepared pans. Repeat with remaining dough. Cover. Let rise in warm place,
free from drafts, for about 45 minutes or until doubled. Preheat oven to 375°.
Bake for about 15 to 20 minutes or until golden brown. Brush lightly with
melted butter. Makes about 2 dozen rolls.

Chocolate Chip Date Cake

Not only is this a great cake, it also comes with a topping the family will enjoy.

Nonstick spray coating
1 cup chopped dates
1 teaspoon baking soda
1 1/4 cups boiling water
2 cups all-purpose flour
1 teaspoon baking powder
1 teaspoon salt

3/4 cup shortening
1 cup granulated sugar
2 beaten eggs
1/2 cup packed brown sugar
1/2 cup chopped walnuts
1 cup chocolate chips

Preheat oven to 350°. Spray a 13 x 9 x 2-inch baking pan with nonstick spray coating. In a medium mixing bowl, combine dates and baking soda. Pour boiling water over dates; stir to mix well. Set aside to cool. In a small bowl, combine flour, baking powder, and salt. In a large mixing bowl, cream together shortening and granulated sugar until light and fluffy. Beat in eggs. Add flour mixture to date mixture, stirring until all the flour is moistened. Stir all into the shortening mixture, beating until well blended. Pour batter into prepared baking pan. In a small bowl, combine brown sugar, walnuts, and chocolate chips; mix well. Sprinkle brown sugar mixture evenly over cake batter. Bake for 40 to 45 minutes or until toothpick inserted into center comes out clean. Makes about 12 to 15 servings.

Grandma K's Cherry Cake

Let this cake rest overnight to allow the spicy flavor and moisture to develop.

1 cup flour
1 teaspoon baking soda
1 teaspoon ground cinnamon
1/2 teaspoon ground nutmeg
1/2 teaspoon salt
1/4 cup shortening
1 cup sugar

2 eggs
1 cup canned, pitted, tart cherries,
    drained
1/2 cup thick sour milk or buttermilk
Powdered sugar icing, optional (see
    recipe, below)

Preheat oven to 350°. Grease and lightly flour a 13 x 9 x 2-inch baking pan. In a medium bowl, combine flour, baking soda, cinnamon, nutmeg, and salt; mix well. In a large mixing bowl, cream shortening. Add sugar gradually; cream until light and fluffy. Add eggs, one at a time; beat thoroughly after each addition. Blend in cherries. Add dry ingredients and sour milk to batter, mixing well. Pour into prepared pan. Bake for 40 to 45 minutes or until toothpick inserted in center comes out dry and clean. Cool. Frost with your favorite powdered sugar icing, if desired. Makes 12 to 15 servings.

Powdered Sugar Frosting

Aunt Margaret's original frosting recipe called for cream, but I found that milk works just as well.

2 cups powdered sugar
4 tablespoons butter, softened
4 tablespoons cream
1/2 teaspoon vanilla

In a medium bowl, combine sugar and butter; beat until well blended. Stir in cream and vanilla and stir until smooth. Mixture should be thin. Makes about 2 cups, or enough to frost a 13 x 9 x 2-inch cake.

Horseradish: Something to Cry About

Recipes in This Chapter

Mother began weeping midmorning. By noon she was still sitting on the back porch with tears streaming down her cheeks. In the middle of the afternoon, she moved to the north porch to sit with the wind at her back. The sun couldn't reach her there, but that didn't stop the tears.

It hurt to see my mother cry like that especially when I knew it was my father's fault. Well—almost his fault. Mother also liked horseradish. In fact, we all did.

When we moved to our new farm in early March, Dad found a hearty horseradish patch out behind the woodshed. You'd think he found a hidden treasure. As soon as the frost was pretty well out of the ground, he picked a sunny day with a brisk wind and armed himself with a spade and a basket.

When he returned, Mom and Dad formed an assembly line to wash, cut, peel, scrape, and scour the horseradish roots in warm water. Dad screwed the food grinder to the seat of an old kitchen chair. Mom bravely stuck a long farmer's match in her mouth (someone once told her it would help keep the fumes out of her face). Within minutes, tears ran down her cheeks and she tossed the match aside.

Joe, a neighbor, stopped by. After

several minutes, he suggested that my mother tie a cloth over her nose, bandit-style. The tears kept flowing. By now her nose looked like a red rubber ball and her eyes were puffy and swollen.

Dad hovered, watching and directing her progress. "Must be good stuff, if it's making you cry like that," he said.

Reaching for another root, she glared up at him. "Anytime you want to trade places," she sniffed. The men disappeared before she finished speaking.

Once Mother ground the roots, she measured out $1/2$ cup of vinegar for each cup of horseradish, added a little salt and a bit of sugar, and ladled the mixture into $1/2$-pint jars. She sealed the jars tightly and left them on the kitchen counter along with a covered dish of fresh homemade horseradish for supper.

When Dad and Joe returned to the house, Dad beamed at her display. Dipping a small spoon into the dish of horseradish, he savored a taste. He gulped and his eyes became teary, but he kept on smiling. Obviously, the current batch met with his approval.

"Now this is prime. It's fresh and zesty just like homemade horseradish is meant to be." Dad liked his horseradish eye-rolling and sinus-clearing hot. Grinding horseradish in early spring assured him of that.

"Fall grinding is too mild," he insisted to Joe. "Here, have a nip." Dad dipped the tip of a spoon into the horseradish and offered it to his unsuspecting friend.

"Egads, man, you must have a galvanized gullet to eat that," Joe sputtered when he recovered his breath and wiped off the sweat beading on his forehead. "That stuff is really HOT."

"Homemade horseradish will cure any sinus condition you have," Dad said.

I noticed Joe didn't refuse the jar of fresh horseradish Dad offered when he left for home.

For the next several weeks, the horseradish container appeared on the table along with the salt and pepper shakers. Dad used it like mustard, spreading it on his fish and meat. In fact, he ate it on everything except pie, cakes, cookies, and puddings. Mother, a bit more selective, enjoyed a touch on her breakfast eggs and fried potatoes at supper. She added some to her tomato sauces and creamed vegetable dishes.

No one ever insisted that my brothers and I sample horseradish. We simply followed our parents' examples. We ignored the itch in our noses, the dripping sinuses and the tears rolling down our cheeks. After all, homemade horseradish was something worth crying about.

Zesty Horseradish Meat Loaf

Horseradish lends a savory touch to our favorite meat loaf.

Nonstick spray coating
2/3 cup crushed cornflake crumbs
1 slightly beaten egg
1 tablespoon Worcestershire sauce
3/4 cup tomato juice
1/2 cup finely chopped onion
1/4 cup snipped parsley

1 teaspoon salt
1 teaspoon dry mustard
1/8 teaspoon pepper
1/4 cup prepared horseradish
1 1/2 pounds lean ground beef

Preheat oven to 350°. Spray a 9 x 5 x 3–inch loaf pan with nonstick spray coating. In a large mixing bowl, combine crushed cornflakes, egg, Worcestershire sauce, tomato juice, onion, parsley, salt, mustard, and pepper; beat until well mixed. Blend in horseradish. Stir in ground beef until well mixed. Press meat mixture evenly into prepared loaf pan. Bake for 55 to 60 minutes or until well browned and thoroughly done. Makes about 6 to 8 servings.

Grandma Mary's Horseradish Gravy

This variation of milk gravy is not sharp, but it does have a wonderful, delicate flavor when served over beef roast.

2 tablespoons butter or margarine
2 tablespoons all-purpose flour
1/8 teaspoon salt
Dash of white pepper
3 cups milk
3 tablespoons prepared horseradish, or to taste

In a small saucepan, melt butter. Stir in flour, salt, and pepper. Add milk. Cook and stir with a wire whisk over medium heat for 8 to 10 minutes or until thick and bubbly. Stir in horseradish. Cook and stir for 4 to 5 more minutes. Serve warm. Makes about 3 cups.

Horseradish Sauce

A nippy horseradish sauce to complement a meat loaf or sliced tongue sandwich.

1 cup sour cream
1 tablespoon milk
1/4 cup prepared horseradish, or to taste
1 tablespoon chopped chives
1/2 teaspoon salt

In a small mixing bowl, combine sour cream, milk, horseradish, chives, and salt. Stir until well mixed. Cover and refrigerate. Serve chilled. Makes about 1 1/4 cups.

Horseradish-Flavored Potato Salad

If you enjoy the nippy taste of horseradish, you'll appreciate the distinctive flavor it lends to potato salad.

6 or 7 medium potatoes, cooked in jackets
1/2 cup salad oil
2 tablespoons cider vinegar
1 teaspoon salt
Dash of pepper
1 cup mayonnaise

4 hard-boiled eggs, sliced
1/2 cup sour cream
1/2 cup minced onion
3/4 cup diced celery
1 tablespoon snipped parsley
2 tablespoons prepared horseradish

Slip the skins off cooked potatoes as soon as cool enough to handle. Dice potatoes into a large bowl. In a small bowl, combine oil, vinegar, salt, and pepper; blend thoroughly. Pour 1/3 of the oil mixture over potatoes. Let stand at least 1 hour. Add mayonnaise, eggs, sour cream, onion, celery, parsley, and horseradish to remaining oil mixture; mix well. Pour over potato mixture. Stir gently to blend. Chill until ready to serve. Makes about 6 to 8 servings.

Beets with Horseradish and Sour Cream

The contrast of flavors is what brings out the best in beets and makes this a tasty dish. Serve it with any main course.

3 tablespoons butter or margarine
1/2 cup minced onion
3 tablespoons all-purpose flour
1 1/2 cups chicken broth
1/2 cup sour cream
3 tablespoons prepared horseradish

3 cups diced beets
1/2 teaspoon salt
1/8 teaspoon freshly ground pepper
1–2 thinly sliced green onions, for garnish

In a large skillet, melt butter over medium heat and sauté the minced onions, stirring occasionally for 3 minutes or until they just begin to turn golden. Stir in the flour. Gradually add chicken broth. Blend until smooth, stirring until mixture bubbles and thickens. Remove from heat. Blend in sour cream, horseradish, and beets. Season to taste with salt and pepper. Gently toss to coat beets. Return to heat. Simmer over low heat until beets are thoroughly heated; do not boil. Serve warm, garnished with a sprinkling of sliced green onions. Makes about 6 to 8 servings.

Roast Beef-Horseradish Sandwich Filling

A perfect way to turn cold leftover roast beef into a moist sandwich filling— especially when paired with fresh homemade bread.

1 1/2 cups shredded cooked roast beef
1/2 cup diced green pepper
1/4 cup minced onion
4–6 tablespoons mayonnaise

2 tablespoons prepared horseradish, or to taste
Salt, to taste
Pepper, to taste

In a medium mixing bowl, combine roast beef, green pepper, and onion. Stir in just enough mayonnaise to moisten. Add horseradish. Season with salt and pepper. Serve cold. Makes about 2 1/2 cups.

NOTE: You can replace roast beef with equal amounts of shredded cooked pork roast or chopped cooked corned beef.

A Country-Style Easter

Recipes In This Chapter

Easter was like no other time in Mother's country kitchen. It was a holy day, and held an exciting freshness, a born-again feeling unique to this holiday.

Since Mother held to many of her mother's European food customs while adding some of her own, Easter was filled with special foods. Aside from a regular menu, special breads, colored eggs, and ham were always on her Easter menu.

Our favorite Easter kitchen tradition centered on ham—preferably home-cured and hickory-smoked in Father's smokehouse—and at least six dozen eggs. Sometimes Mother used eight dozen. She boiled the hickory-smoked ham for at least an hour in a 20-quart kettle, then let it cool in the liquid. While it cooled, we washed the eggs and let them warm to room temperature.

After the ham cooled, she removed it from the liquid and carefully added the eggs to the ham broth. The ham liquid and eggs were returned to the heat and kept at a low boil for about a half hour. She then let the eggs cool in the ham broth.

"This is important," she stressed, "to draw in the ham's smoky flavor."

Some claimed they couldn't taste any hint of ham in the hard-boiled eggs. However, if you ate one plain boiled and then one of Mom's Easter eggs, you noticed the delightful difference. We enjoyed the ham-flavored eggs so much we nibbled and snacked on them between meals rather than eating candy.

While she tended the boiling eggs, Mother repeated age-old egg-related legends and myths she'd heard, I'm sure from her own mother.

"Some say," she began, "if you find two yolks in an Easter egg, that is a sign of coming financial prosperity. If you refuse an Easter egg you endanger your friendship with the person offering it."

"And," she went on, "Easter eggs cooked on Good Friday will promote fertility of trees and crops and protect against a sudden death."

"In some parts of Europe," she continued, "it's a legend that eggs laid on Good Friday, if kept for a hundred years, will have their yolks turn to diamonds."

When I laughed at the idea of eggs turning to diamonds, she scolded me. "Eggs are the symbol of spring fertility and new life. They deserve respect."

Between boiling the ham and eggs (which usually took up most of the day) and baking an assortment of special breads, the kitchen filled with rich, tantalizing aromas that teased and taunted us all day long into begging for just a taste to supplement our meager meals. (A strict traditionalist, Mother insisted that the Lenten fasting continue until Easter Sunday morning.)

At last, Easter Sunday morning arrived. After we'd found our candy-filled baskets, the plates of braided egg bread rings and bunny rolls on the breakfast table next to the platters of ham and ham-flavored eggs made all the waiting worthwhile.

Basic Sweet Yeast Dough

Mother discovered this recipe in one of my 4-H Foods Project Bulletins. Versatile and easy to work with, it quickly became her favorite recipe for all types of baking calling for sweet yeast dough.

1/2 cup warm water
2 packages active dry yeast
2 cups milk
1 cup butter or margarine
1/2 cup sugar

2 teaspoons salt
2 beaten eggs
8–8 1/2 cups all-purpose flour, divided
Melted butter, as needed

In a small bowl, combine warm water and yeast. Allow to stand 5 minutes or until yeast is softened. In a saucepan, heat milk to warm (120° to 130°). In a large mixing bowl, combine butter, sugar, and salt. Stir milk into sugar mixture and continue stirring until butter melts. Add eggs, dissolved yeast, and 3–3 1/2 cups of flour; beat well. Gradually work in 2 1/2–3 cups more flour. Turn dough out onto a lightly floured surface and knead in enough of the remaining flour to make a smooth, satiny dough, for about 8 to 10 minutes. Turn into a buttered bowl and brush top of dough with melted butter. Cover and let rise until doubled, about 1 to 1 1/2 hours. Punch dough down and turn out onto a lightly floured surface again. Divide dough in half and proceed to follow recipes for bunny rolls or ham buns.

Ham Buns

These are light and tender—perfect for ham sandwiches. They also freeze well.

Nonstick spray coating
Basic sweet yeast dough (see recipe, page 31)
Melted butter, as needed

Spray a 15 1/2 x 12-inch baking sheet with nonstick spray coating. When basic sweet yeast dough is ready to use, divide into quarters. Lightly knead a single quarter, then roll or pat to a thickness of 1/2 to 3/4 inch. Cut into rolls with either a round doughnut cutter or a heavy glass of desired width. Place rolls on prepared sheets. Cover and let rise again until doubled. Meanwhile, preheat oven to 400°. Before baking, brush with melted butter. Bake for 15 to 20 minutes or until browned on both sides. Remove from oven and cool on wire racks. Makes about 24 buns, depending on size.

Bunny Faces

The kids will love these.

    Nonstick spray coating
    Basic sweet yeast dough (see recipe, page 31)
    Glaze*
    Shredded coconut

Spray a 15 1/2 x 12-inch baking sheet with nonstick spray coating. When basic sweet yeast dough is ready to use, divide into balls the size of a large egg. Roll each under hands on lightly floured surface to form a long strand 1/2 inch in diameter. Let rest 5 minutes. Cut strands into 10-inch lengths. Tie each length into a loose knot, bringing ends up to form bunny ears. Place 3 inches apart on prepared pans and cover. Let rise for 30 minutes or until doubled. Meanwhile, preheat oven to 375°. Bake for about 15 to 20 minutes or until lightly browned. (Watch carefully so they do not overbrown.) Remove from oven and cool on wire racks. To decorate, press glaze through a small tip of a decorating set or a small hole cut into a waxed-paper cone and outline ears, eyes, and nose. Press coconut into glaze for whiskers. Makes about 1 1/2 dozen bunny faces, depending on the amount of dough used in each face.

*Glaze

In a small mixing bowl, combine 1 cup powdered sugar with about 1 tablespoon milk and 1/4 teaspoon vanilla; beat until smooth. Put 2 tablespoons of glaze into a small bowl. Add several small drops of red food coloring to tint for bunny features. Spread a thin coating of uncolored glaze on the still-warm bunny faces. Use the tinted glaze to add the facial features.

Twisted Easter Egg Bread Rings

The baked ring seems to have eggs resting in the nest. This is an attractive wreath, with or without the powdered sugar frosting.

Nonstick spray coating
1/2 cup milk
1/2 cup sugar
1/2 cup butter
1 teaspoon salt
Grated peel of 2 lemons
2 packages active dry yeast

1/2 cup warm water
2 beaten eggs
4 1/2–5 cups all-purpose flour, divided
12 colored raw eggs in shell
1 beaten egg
Powdered sugar frosting*

Spray a large bowl with nonstick spray coating. In a saucepan, combine milk, sugar, butter, salt, and lemon peel and heat until warm (120° to 130°) and butter is almost melted. In a small bowl, dissolve yeast in warm water. Add to milk mixture with eggs and 2–2 1/2 cups flour; beat until smooth. Stir in enough remaining flour, a little at a time, to form a dough that is easy to handle. Turn out onto lightly floured board and knead until smooth and elastic for about 5 to 8 minutes. Place in prepared bowl; turn dough over to grease top. Cover and let rise in warm place for 45 minutes or until doubled. Punch down and let rise again. Spray two 15 1/2 x 12-inch baking sheets with nonstick spray coating. Turn out onto lightly floured surface and divide dough into 4 equal parts. Form each part into a 16-inch rope. Shape 2 of the ropes on prepared baking sheet into a very loosely twisted ring, leaving space for 6 eggs. Repeat with other rope of dough for the second ring. Insert colored raw eggs into each ring. Cover and let rise about 30 minutes or until doubled. Preheat oven to 375°. Brush rings evenly with beaten egg. Bake for 20 minutes or until lightly browned. Remove from oven and cool on wire rack. Frost with powdered sugar frosting*. Makes 2 rings.

*Powdered Sugar Frosting

In a small bowl, combine 1 1/2 cups of powdered sugar with about 1 tablespoon milk, 1/4 teaspoon vanilla, and a pinch of salt. Beat until smooth.

Goldenrod Eggs

Attractive, tasty, and great for a light after-Easter lunch or supper.

8 hard-boiled eggs	2 cups milk
1/4 cup butter	1 15-ounce can peas, drained
1/4 cup all-purpose flour	4 slices bread, toasted
1/2 teaspoon salt	Paprika for garnish, optional
1/4 teaspoon pepper	

Separate egg whites and yolks. Press yolks through a sieve into a small bowl; set aside. Chop egg whites into a small bowl; set aside. In a medium saucepan, melt butter over medium-high heat. Stir in flour, salt, and pepper. Cook, stirring constantly, until mixture is smooth and bubbly. Gradually stir in milk. Cook, stirring constantly, until mixture boils and thickens. Add peas and chopped egg whites; blend into white sauce mixture. Continue cooking and stirring until peas are heated through. Remove from heat. Arrange toast slices on serving plates. Spoon 1/4 cup egg mixture over toast. Sprinkle 1/4 cup of sieved egg yolks over each slice of toast. Dust with a dash of paprika, if desired. Serve immediately. Makes 4 servings.

Lemon Meringue Pie

Mention lemon meringue pie to anyone in our family and we instantly think of Mother. It was her signature dish, the one dessert we requested she bring to all family dinners. The extra-flaky crust with its pleasantly tart lemon filling hiding under a lightly browned meringue crown was heavenly. I've often tried to duplicate her recipe, but, as I've mentioned, it was her signature dish. So it remains a loving memory of Mother's baking talents.

Baked 9-inch pastry shell
  (see recipe, page 37)
1 cup sugar
1/4 cup plus 2 tablespoons cornstarch
Dash of salt
1 1/3 cups cold water

3 slightly beaten extra-large egg yolks
1/4 cup freshly squeezed lemon juice
1 tablespoon butter
2 teaspoons finely grated lemon peel
Meringue for 9-inch pie (see recipe, page 37)

In a medium saucepan, combine sugar, cornstarch, and salt. Blend in water gradually; stir until well mixed. Cook over medium-high heat, stirring constantly, until thickened and bubbly. Reduce heat and cook for 2 more minutes. Remove from heat. Gradually combine 1/2 cup of hot mixture with egg yolks, then quickly blend in. Add this mixture and lemon juice to remaining cornstarch mixture; mix thoroughly. Bring mixture to a low boil; cook for 2 minutes, stirring constantly. Remove saucepan from the heat. Add butter and lemon peel; stir vigorously until well blended. Let the mixture cool only slightly before pouring into flaky pastry shell. Smooth the meringue over the lemon filling and bake according to the meringue recipe. Remove from oven and cool on wire rack. Makes one 9-inch pie.

Meringue

3 large egg whites, at room temperature
1/4 teaspoon cream of tartar
Dash of salt
1/4 cup plus 2 tablespoons sugar

Preheat oven to 350°. In a large mixing bowl, beat egg whites with an electric mixer on high speed until foamy. Add cream of tartar and salt. Continue beating until soft peaks hold. Gradually add sugar, 1 tablespoon at a time, and continue beating on high speed until mixture forms stiff, glossy peaks. Immediately spread meringue evenly over lemon filling to the edges of the crust to seal it and prevent shrinking. Shape the meringue into medium-high peaks with the back of a spoon. Bake for 5 minutes. Reduce heat to 325° and continue baking for 7 to 10 minutes or until the meringue is golden. Remove from oven and cool on wire rack. Makes topping for one 9-inch lemon meringue pie.

Flaky Pastry (for Single Crust)

1 1/2 cups all-purpose flour
1/2 teaspoon salt
1/2 cup shortening
4–5 tablespoons cold water

In a mixing bowl, combine flour and salt. Cut in shortening until pieces are the size of small peas. Sprinkle with water, 1 tablespoon at a time, tossing mixture after each addition. Repeat until mixture is moistened. Form dough into a ball. On a lightly floured surface, turn out dough and flatten with hands. With a rolling pin, roll from the center out to a 1/8-inch thickness, forming a circle slightly larger than the pie plate. Wrap pastry around rolling pin and lift into place onto pie plate. Ease into place, being careful not to tear. Trim the dough even with pie plate. Makes enough pastry for one 10-inch single-crust pie.

Stalking the Wild Asparagus

Recipes in This Chapter

The best way to gather wild asparagus is to take a small child by the hand and leisurely walk the farm fence lines. You will rediscover the wonders of nature while eager young eyes will discover the joys of finding the tender green spears hidden beneath last year's dried ferns.

One of the tremendous benefits of country living in the spring is picking wild asparagus. In fact, I hold my breath each spring not quite believing the season is here until I see the delicate green shoots peeping out to greet the sunshine. Then I know spring is here. For, if the ground is warm enough for the asparagus to grow, it is warm enough to plant the garden.

I have a lingering love affair with asparagus stalking going back to my grade school days. At the first sign of spring I kept a close lookout, while walking home from school, for the awakening shoots growing along the roadsides. I picked the wild asparagus as fast as it grew. Of course, I had my secret asparagus patches along fence lines and around an old farmstead. I even took my bike and rode down back roads and lanes looking for new beds.

There is only one trouble with combing the ditches in unfamiliar territory. That was the danger of the lurking poison ivy plants. For as sure as spring and new asparagus, I came home with the dreaded rash. I recall sitting in the vile weed when I was in the third grade. I didn't learn much from that, as I picked up another severe case when I was a senior in high school. I can still hear Mother scolding, "Not again."

Asparagus hunting is in my blood. A tear still comes to my eye when I recall the township roadbeds being reworked. There is no doubting the wisdom of town officials destroying the poison ivy, but not my asparagus beds!

During the all-too-short wild asparagus season, Mother found a number of delicious ways to serve the harvest I brought home. Many of the dishes I still prepare today. However, my family believes there is nothing to compare with fresh asparagus cooked until just tender—not limp—covered with milk and swimming in pools of melted butter and served over mashed potatoes, biscuits or toast. It's not a very sophisticated dish, but one to win praises for country cooks.

Creamy Asparagus

A quick and simple dish for family dinners or unexpected guests.

2 pounds fresh asparagus spears
2 cups sour cream
1/2 cup grated Parmesan cheese
1/2 teaspoon garlic salt
Paprika for garnish, optional

Wash asparagus and snap off woody ends. In a medium saucepan, cook asparagus in lightly salted water until crisp-tender. Drain. In a medium bowl, combine sour cream, cheese, and garlic salt; stir until well blended. Arrange hot asparagus on serving dish. Top with sour cream mixture. Garnish with a light sprinkle of paprika, if desired. Makes about 4 to 6 servings.

Asparagus and Egg Salad

This tasty combination of asparagus and eggs is especially attractive when served on plates lined with lettuce leaves and garnished with red pepper rings.

1 1/2 pounds asparagus
1/2 cup water
6 hard-boiled eggs
1/4 cup diced red onion
1/2 cup mayonnaise
1 tablespoon milk
2 teaspoons cider vinegar

1 teaspoon sugar
Salt, to taste
Freshly ground pepper, to taste
Dash paprika for garnish, optional
Lettuce leaves for garnish, optional
Red pepper rings for garnish, optional

Wash asparagus and snap off woody ends. Cut each spear into 1-inch lengths; there should be about 3–4 cups. In a medium saucepan, combine asparagus and water; cover and bring to a boil over high heat. Lower heat and simmer for 5 minutes or until asparagus is crisp-tender. Drain. Rinse asparagus under cold water. Chill. Slice egg into quarters. In a large bowl, combine asparagus, eggs, and onion; toss lightly to blend. In a small bowl, combine mayonnaise, milk, vinegar, sugar, salt, and pepper; mix until well blended. Pour over asparagus mixture. Serve chilled. Arrange the salad in a serving bowl and sprinkle with paprika if desired, or line serving plates with lettuce leaves and garnish with red pepper rings if desired. Makes about 6 servings.

Asparagus with Carrots

Asparagus and carrots are attractive and tasty when served together. They make an excellent side dish for any roast.

1/2 pound asparagus
5 carrots, trimmed and scraped
1 cup water
1/3 cup finely minced green onion

1 tablespoon butter
Salt, to taste
Freshly ground pepper, to taste
Dash of nutmeg, for garnish

Wash asparagus and snap off woody ends. Cut each spear into 1-inch lengths; there should be about 2 cups. Cut each carrot into 1/4-inch rounds; there should be about 2 cups. In a medium saucepan, combine carrots and water; bring to a boil over high heat. Reduce heat to low. Cover and simmer about 6 minutes or until carrots are crisp-tender. Add asparagus. Cover and continue to simmer about 4 to 5 minutes or until asparagus is crisp-tender. Drain. Add green onions and butter. Season with salt and pepper. Stir gently to blend. Garnish with nutmeg. Makes about 4 to 5 servings.

Sweet and Savory Asparagus

This recipe is quick to prepare. The addition of sesame seeds and soy sauce gives asparagus a slightly Asian flavor.

1 pound fresh asparagus
1 tablespoon salad oil
1 cup water
3 tablespoons sugar
2 tablespoons cider vinegar, or to taste

1 teaspoon salt
2 tablespoons cornstarch
1/4 cup water
2 teaspoons sesame seeds
1/2 teaspoon soy sauce, or to taste

Wash asparagus and snap off woody ends. Cut diagonally into 1-inch pieces. Preheat a large heavy skillet over moderate heat. Add asparagus and oil. Cook for about 5 minutes, stirring constantly to coat asparagus with oil. Add 1 cup water, sugar, vinegar, and salt; bring mixture to a boil. Cover and cook for about 10 minutes or until asparagus is tender. In a small bowl, combine cornstarch, 1/4 cup water, sesame seeds, and soy sauce; blend until smooth. Add to asparagus mixture. Cook for 2 to 3 minutes, stirring constantly until sauce thickens. Serve immediately. Makes about 4 to 6 servings.

Cheesy Asparagus Strata

An easy, make-ahead, busy-day dish. Serve with a green salad and vinaigrette dressing.

Nonstick spray coating
7 slices white bread
1 pound fresh asparagus
2 cups shredded sharp cheddar
    cheese
2 cups milk

3 slightly beaten eggs
2 tablespoons melted butter
1 teaspoon salt
$1/2$ teaspoon dry mustard
$1/4$ teaspoon ground thyme

Spray a 12 x 9 x 2-inch baking pan with nonstick spray coating. Stack bread. Cut off crusts and cut into thirds. Lay strips of bread, one layer only, in prepared baking pan. Wash asparagus and snap off woody ends. Cut off tips. Cut stalks into 1-inch pieces. Place asparagus tips and pieces on top of bread. Sprinkle cheese over top. In a medium bowl, combine milk, eggs, butter, salt, dry mustard, and thyme; beat until well blended. Pour over bread and asparagus mixture. Cover. Chill in refrigerator for 2 to 24 hours. Bake uncovered in preheated 325° oven for 50 to 60 minutes or until golden brown and knife inserted in center comes out clean. Let stand for 10 minutes. Makes about 6 to 8 servings.

Asparagus and Chicken Soup

Serve this creamy soup as a main dish or as a side dish.

2 pounds fresh asparagus
1 tablespoon butter or margarine, divided
1/4 cup minced onion
1/4 cup chopped fresh parsley
1 teaspoon ground coriander
1 tablespoon all-purpose flour

2 1/2 cups chicken broth
2 cups cubed cooked chicken or turkey
1/2 cup milk
2–3 teaspoons lemon juice
Pepper, to taste
Lemon slices for garnish, optional

Wash asparagus and snap off woody ends. In a large saucepan, cook asparagus, covered, in boiling water 8 to 10 minutes or until tender. Drain. Cut about 2 inches from tops and reserve. Set spears aside. In a heavy skillet, melt butter over medium-high heat. Add onion, parsley, and coriander and sauté until onion is tender. Reduce heat to low. Add flour and cook for 1 minute, stirring constantly. Gradually add broth and continue cooking over medium heat 4 to 5 minutes longer, stirring constantly. Remove from heat. Add the reserved asparagus spears to broth. Pour asparagus mixture into blender; process until mixture is smooth. Pour mixture into heavy saucepan. Stir in cubed chicken, milk, and reserved asparagus tips. Add lemon juice and pepper. Cook over medium heat until heated thoroughly. Garnish with lemon slices, if desired. Makes about 4 to 6 servings.

Planting Time

Recipes in This Chapter

Spring generally arrived at our farm with a mixed bag of blessings. I couldn't help noticing that by the end of March, spring fever always hit my parents with a vengeance. Of course, they each had their own set of symptoms.

"Most farmers look that way in early spring," Mother told me when I questioned the frown on Dad's face. Several weeks later, he repeated almost the same words when I mentioned Mother needed some cleaning supplies the next time we made a trip to town.

For weeks I kept a close eye on them, but it didn't help. Each day Dad checked his field. One day, he'd pray for April showers to help settle the ground. When the rains came, he prayed for the skies to clear so he could plant his oats. In between, he tinkered with the tractor, planter, or anything to avoid the house.

Mother had her own agenda. She called it "spring cleaning," and Dad wanted no part of it. Some days he wasn't so lucky.

Mother waited to start her cleaning until we no longer needed the large Round Oak heater to take the chill off the house.

"Time to move the heater to the back porch," she announced at breakfast.

Dad didn't look too happy, but he managed a "Guess so."

Once I spread a trail of newspapers across the dining room floor, I kept my distance and watched. Dad and the hired man gently eased the black pipes loose from the wall and lifted them out of the stove connection. They each held a section. Ever so cautiously they headed toward the outside door.

"Be careful," Mother fretted.

"Easy does it," Dad warned.

The hired man didn't say anything.

"Watch where you're going," Mother warned.

Just before Dad reached the doorway, some outside noise distracted him and the back of his pipe jolted into the door frame. His sudden stop surprised the hired man, who in turn bumped into him and dropped his section of pipe. Clouds of black, greasy soot spewed across the room.

Mother gasped and scolded. The mess earned the men a cold shoulder all the while they worked at cleaning it up.

"Just about every year something like that happens," she told me later. "I should be used to it, but I don't have to like it."

Once the mess was cleared, the curtains came down and the furniture was moved out, piece by piece, and then back into each room being cleaned. Mother started in the front room, shifted to the upstairs bedrooms, then back downstairs to the dining room, and finished in the kitchen.

There were times it seemed that every rug, blanket, pillow, and cushion were on the clotheslines sagging with the heavy loads.

"I don't understand why everything has to be hung up and aired," I complained. Mother ignored my grumbling and sent me out with another load.

For some unexplained reason, at spring cleaning time Mother always decided to wallpaper the kitchen walls. Once Dad heard her intentions, he disappeared from the machine shed to fix a fence at the far end of the farm. Meals became a hit-and-miss affair and the kitchen smelled like a room full of schoolhouse paste. So we didn't really blame him.

By the time we finished spring cleaning, the sun had dried up the field enough for the men to work the land. The sound of hustling and the humming of tractors working the fields became an everyday occurrence.

While we had fretted about the weather, grumbled and groaned about the cleaning, Mother Nature kept her own planting schedule. Dad wore a smile as big as his dinner plate and Mother was once again cooking for a hungry crew.

That always made her smile.

Beef Roast with Onions

Most of our main meals started with home-raised beef prepared in a number
of different ways. However, Mother's favorite standby on a busy day—roast
beef—couldn't be beat.

2 tablespoons shortening	Pepper
4- to 6-pound round rump or	2–3 medium onions, peeled and
boneless chuck roast	sliced 1/4 inch thick
Salt	Tomato gravy (see recipe, page 47)

Preheat oven to 325°. In a heavy roasting pan on top of the stove, melt
shortening over medium heat. Brown roast evenly on all sides. (Browning
slowly keeps the meat from drying on the outside. The deeper the browning,
the more tempting the color of the finished roast.) Position the meat in
roasting pan. Season with salt and pepper. Arrange slices of onions on top and
pin in place with toothpicks. Insert roast meat thermometer so it reaches
center of thickest part, making sure that the bulb doesn't rest in fat or touch
bone. Do not add water. Do not cover. Place in preheated oven. Baste
frequently with juices that cook out of the meat. Roast for about 2 1/2 to 3
hours or until desired degree of doneness*. Remove the roast to a hot platter.
For easier carving, allow the roast to "stand" in a warm place 15 to 20 minutes
after removed from oven. Remove toothpicks from onions. Arrange onion slices
around the carved roast. Serve warm with tomato gravy. Makes about 8 to 12
servings.

*After years of country kitchen cooking, Mother "knew" how to tell when her
roast was done just the way the family liked it. For the rest of us, I
recommend using a meat thermometer. Insert the meat thermometer into the
thickest part of the roast. Roast in a slow oven (325°) to the desired degree of
doneness: 140° for rare, 160° for medium, and 170° for well done.

Tomato Gravy

2 tablespoons fat from roasting pan
2 tablespoons all-purpose flour
1 cup tomato juice
1 cup water
Salt, to taste
Pepper, to taste

Pour all but 2 tablespoons of fat from roasting pan. Sprinkle flour into pan; blend into fat. Cook over medium-high heat, stirring constantly until slightly browned. Blend in tomato juice and water. Bring to a boil, stirring constantly. Lower heat and, while stirring, simmer for 5 minutes or until mixture is thickened and thoroughly heated. Season with salt and pepper. Serve warm over beef roast with onions or and mashed potatoes. Makes about 2 cups.

Wilted Lettuce and Bacon Salad

This old-fashioned salad is best made with fresh-picked leaf lettuce.

6 slices bacon, chopped
3 tablespoons bacon fat
1/2 cup cider vinegar
2 tablespoons water
3 teaspoons sugar, or to taste
1/2 teaspoon salt
1/8 teaspoon pepper
1/2 cup chopped onion
Leaf lettuce, freshly picked and cleaned, enough to fill a large salad bowl

In a heavy skillet, fry bacon pieces until crisp and lightly browned. Using a slotted spoon, remove bacon and drain on a paper towel. Cover to keep warm. Drain off all but 3 tablespoons of bacon fat. In a small bowl, combine vinegar, water, sugar, salt, and pepper; beat well to blend. Sprinkle onions and bacon over lettuce. Carefully stir vinegar mixture into the bacon fat in skillet. Place skillet over high heat and bring the mixture to a boil. Adjust seasonings to taste. Remove from heat and pour over lettuce. Toss lightly to coat lettuce. Serve immediately. Makes about 6 servings.

Glazed Carrots and Onions

Whenever Mother prepared this buttery vegetable dish, she had no problem getting us to eat our carrots.

6 medium carrots	2 teaspoons paprika
1/4 cup butter or margarine	1 teaspoon sugar
2–3 medium onions, peeled and quartered	1/2 teaspoon salt
2 teaspoons snipped parsley	1/4 teaspoon pepper
	3–4 tablespoons water

Scrape the carrots and cut into 1/4-inch slices. In a large saucepan, melt butter over medium heat. Add carrots, onions, parsley, paprika, sugar, salt, and pepper to butter. Cover with a tight-fitting lid and braise for about 15 to 20 minutes or until carrots are just tender, stirring occasionally to coat evenly and prevent scorching. Add water and taste for seasoning. Cover and continue to cook over low heat. When all the liquid is absorbed, the vegetables are ready to serve warm with roast beef or pork. Makes about 4 to 6 servings.

Old-Fashioned Rice Pudding

Easy to prepare and versatile, rice pudding blends well with raisins, a number of fresh fruit toppings, fruit preserves, or drained crushed pineapple. For best results, be sure to use long-grain rice.

3 cups cooked long-grain rice	1 teaspoon vanilla
3 cups milk	Ground nutmeg, optional
1/2 cup sugar	Cream, optional
3 tablespoons butter or margarine	

In a medium-heavy saucepan, combine rice, milk, sugar, and butter; stir to blend. Cook over medium heat, stirring often, for 25 to 30 minutes or until thickened. Blend in vanilla. Serve warm or cold, spooned into individual dessert dishes. Sprinkle lightly with nutmeg and pour cream over each serving. Makes about 5 to 6 servings.

Whole Wheat Bread

What could be better than fresh, home-baked whole wheat bread?

2 cups all-purpose flour
2 packages dry yeast
1 cup milk
1 cup water
1/4 cup cooking oil
1/4 cup honey

1 tablespoon salt
1 egg, room temperature
4–4 1/2 cups whole wheat flour
Nonstick spray coating
Melted butter, as needed

In a large mixing bowl, stir together all-purpose flour and yeast. In a small saucepan, heat milk, water, oil, honey, and salt until warm (125° to 130°). Cool to lukewarm. Add liquid ingredients to flour-yeast mixture. Beat with an electric mixer on medium speed for 3 minutes, scraping sides of bowl frequently. Beat in egg. Stir in whole wheat flour to make a moderately stiff dough. Turn onto lightly floured surface, cover with the bowl, and let rest 10 minutes. Knead until smooth and satiny for about 8 to 10 minutes. Cover and let rest 20 minutes. Spray two 8 1/2 x 4 1/2-inch loaf pans with nonstick spray coating. To shape loaves, divide dough in half. Roll each half into a 14 x 7-inch rectangle. Roll up from narrow side, pressing roll into dough at each turn. Press ends to seal and fold under loaf. Place dough in prepared pans. Brush with melted butter. Let rise in warm place until doubled, about 60 to 75 minutes. Preheat oven to 400°. Bake for 35 to 45 minutes or until golden brown and loaves sound hollow when tapped. (If loaves are browning too quickly, cover loosely with foil.) Remove immediately from pans to cool on wire racks. Brush with melted butter. Cool completely before slicing. Makes two 1 1/2-pound loaves.

Applesauce Cookies

This is a spicy, raisin dotted cookie.

Nonstick spray coating
2 cups all-purpose flour
1 teaspoon salt
1 teaspoon cinnamon
1/2 teaspoon allspice
1/2 teaspoon baking soda
1/2 cup shortening, softened

1 cup packed brown sugar
1 slightly beaten egg
1 1/2 cups sweetened canned
   applesauce
1 cup rolled oats
1 cup raisins

Preheat oven to 375°. Spray a 15 x 12-inch cookie sheet with nonstick spray coating. In a medium bowl, combine flour, salt, cinnamon, allspice, and baking soda. In a large mixing bowl, combine shortening and sugar; beat until creamy. Blend in egg and applesauce. (Mixture may separate, but it will blend evenly when dry ingredients are added.) Add flour mixture to creamed mixture, mixing well. Stir in oats and raisins. Drop heaping teaspoonfuls about 2 inches apart onto prepared cookie sheet. Bake for 12 to 15 minutes or until evenly browned. Makes about 5 dozen cookies.

A Country-Style Spring Tonic

Recipes in This Chapter

"A garden isn't much of a garden unless there's a few rhubarb plants somewhere in the back corner." Mother repeated these words each time we moved.

Some called it rhubarb and others called it pie plant, but Mother considered rhubarb the most refreshing spring tonic in her farm garden.

After a long, long winter and slow, slow spring, she'd practically will the lingering March snows to melt and reveal her treasured rhubarb patch. She'd prowl the garden spot looking for signs of its location.

"Are they up yet?" Dad called out to her each morning on his way in from chores.

"Don't see any," she'd answer and continue her searching, day after day, through sunshine and a good share of April showers. Finally she answered his question before he had a chance to ask it: "I found some and it's starting to grow."

Mother's excitement over her find didn't thrill me at all. Everyone in the family liked rhubarb any way she served it. Everyone that is, but me. Just looking at the tender shoots made my jaws pinch and tighten at the thought of its sourness.

I remembered how just the year before my father teased me into tasting a raw, green stalk of rhubarb. We'd been walking in the garden of our old farm when he pulled up a stalk, chopped off the leaf and root end, bit off a piece and chomped away.

"Want a bite?" he offered when he

noticed my horrified expression.

When I hesitated, he cut off a long piece and handed it to me. "Go ahead try it. It really tastes good," he said.

I remember he had a look in his eye I didn't quite understand. However, at six years of age I admired my father: If he said something was good, I believed him. But after that memorable escapade, I refused to sample any and all rhubarb dishes Mother put on the table.

She ignored my scrunched-up nose and went right ahead cooking up the sour stalks. She even put them in breads, coffee cakes, and something she called "fools." Well I'd been fooled once with rhubarb and I didn't intend to let it happen again.

I had no yearning for anything remotely connected to rhubarb until late May of the following spring. I came home from school that day extra hungry. The kitchen was filled with a rich, spicy aroma. Sniffing the air, I looked at Mother. "What did you bake?" I asked.

"Rhubarb custard pie," she answered. "It's a new recipe from the Homemakers' Club."

"It smells . . . kind of good," I reluctantly admitted.

"I'm sure it will be," she smiled and went about preparing supper. When she left the kitchen, I walked over to the cupboard and stared down at the cooling pie. It looked delicious, all golden brown with a light dusting of sugar glistening on the crust. A small bubble of filling oozed out on the edge right in front of me. Looking over my shoulder to check if anyone was watching, I dared to dip my index finger into the center for a little sample.

Surprised, I stared at my finger. It wasn't sour at all. In fact, it tasted sweet and spicy just like it smelled. I eyed the remaining bubble and dared to take just a bit more to be sure my taste buds weren't playing tricks on me.

"Not bad, is it?"

I jumped at the sound of Mother's voice. "I . . . I," stammered. "I was just sampling."

She smiled and gave me a big hug. "I just knew you'd get around to sampling one of my rhubarb dishes sooner or later. How did it taste?"

"Pretty good."

"Of course it is. There's nothing wrong with rhubarb except it needs a lot of sugar."

Later when she served dessert at the evening meal, I surprised everyone by asking for a piece of pie. After that meal, rhubarb was transformed in my mind from sour stalk to Mother's rhubarb pie, kuchen, cake, cobbler, crisp, and, yes, even her "fools" were fantastic. I have to admit I enjoyed them all.

I'll even admit that the next spring I shared her excitement when we found the first ruddy knob. I began to count the days until she'd prepare a whole array of tart and tasty rhubarb desserts. Just like Mother, I couldn't think of a better country-style spring tonic to follow the hearty foods of winter.

Fresh Rhubarb Sauce

A simple country kitchen recipe that's delicious at any meal.

1 1/2 cups rhubarb
1/2 cup water
1/2 cup sugar

In a medium saucepan, combine rhubarb, water, and sugar; stir to blend. Bring to a boil over medium-high heat. Lower heat and simmer, stirring occasionally, for 10 minutes or until rhubarb is tender. Remove from heat and cool. Makes 4 to 5 servings.

NOTES:
• May be served with cream or whipped cream.
• After cooking, add 3/4 cup crushed pineapple.
• Just before removing from heat, add 1 pint of sliced strawberries.

Makes 6 to 8 servings.

Rhubarb-Strawberry Cobbler

You'll want to double this recipe when there's company.

3 cups cut-up rhubarb
1 cup sugar
$1/4$ cup water
1 cup all-purpose flour
2 tablespoons sugar
1 $1/2$ teaspoons baking powder
$1/4$ teaspoon salt
$1/8$ teaspoon baking soda
3 tablespoons butter or margarine

$1/3$ cup plus 1 tablespoon buttermilk
2 cups sliced strawberries
3 tablespoons butter
2 tablespoons water
1 tablespoon cornstarch
1 teaspoon lemon juice
Sweetened whipped cream for
    topping

In a large skillet with a cover, combine rhubarb, sugar, and water. Bring to a boil over medium-high heat. Reduce heat. Cover and simmer for about 5 to 8 minutes or until rhubarb is tender. Meanwhile, in a large bowl, combine flour, sugar, baking powder, salt, and baking soda; stir to blend. Cut in butter until mixture resembles coarse crumbs. Add buttermilk. Mix with a fork until dough clings together; set aside. Stir strawberries and butter into cooked rhubarb. In a small bowl, combine water, cornstarch, and lemon juice; blend until smooth. Stir into rhubarb mixture. Bring to a simmer over medium heat, stirring constantly. Drop biscuit dough by rounded tablespoons onto simmering fruit. Cover and cook for 15 to 18 minutes or until dough is thoroughly baked. Serve warm in bowls topped with whipped cream. Makes about 6 to 8 servings.

Rhubarb Custard Pie

Ideally, rhubarb pie should be served warm with a scoop of vanilla ice cream. But a slice of cooled pie is still a special treat.

Flaky pastry for double-crust pie (see recipe, page 56)
1 1/2 cups sugar
3 tablespoons all-purpose flour
2 tablespoons butter, softened
3/4 teaspoon ground nutmeg

2 well-beaten eggs
3 cups cut-up rhubarb
Milk for garnish on top crust, optional
Sugar for garnish on top crust, optional

Preheat oven to 450°. Prepare pastry and line pie plate with dough. In a large bowl, combine sugar, flour, butter, and nutmeg; stir to blend. Add eggs and beat until smooth. Arrange rhubarb in pie shell. Pour custard batter over rhubarb. Roll out remaining dough into a circle slightly larger than the diameter of the pie plate. Cut decorative slits in the dough. Dampen the edge of the lower crust with water. Roll dough onto a rolling pin to lift over pie plate and settle into place. Seal with fingers. Flute a decorative edge between fingers or with a fork. Lightly brush a fine film of milk over the crust. Dust a sprinkle of sugar over the surface. Place pie on lower shelf of oven. Bake for 15 minutes. Lower heat to 350° and continue baking for 40 to 45 minutes or until crust is lightly browned and juices begin to bubble out. Remove from oven and cool on wire rack. Serve warm or cooled. Makes about 6 to 8 servings.

Flaky Pastry (for Double Crust)

2 cups all-purpose flour
1 teaspoon salt
2/3 cup shortening
5–7 tablespoons cold water

In a mixing bowl, combine flour and salt. Cut in shortening until pieces are the size of peas. Sprinkle water over, 1 tablespoon at a time, tossing mixture after each addition. Repeat until flour mixture is moistened. Form dough into a ball. On a lightly floured surface, turn out dough and flatten with hands. With a rolling pin, roll from the center out to a thickness of $1/8$ inch, forming a circle slightly larger than the pie plate. Wrap pastry around rolling pin and lift into place onto pie plate. Ease into place, being careful not to tear. Trim the dough even with pie plate. Roll out remaining dough on a lightly floured surface slightly larger than pie plate. Roll onto a rolling pin and lift over pie filling and settle into place. Seal with fingers. Flute a decorative edge between fingers or with a fork. Bake as directed in individual recipes.

Rhubarb-Pineapple Custard Kuchen

Guests and family will gobble up this warm-from-the-oven kuchen.

Nonstick spray coating
1/2 cup butter or margarine
1/4 cup sugar
1/2 teaspoon salt
1 egg yolk
1 1/4 cups all-purpose flour
1/4 cup milk (approximately)
2 1/2 cups cooked rhubarb
1 cup drained crushed pineapple

2 eggs
1 egg white
3/4 cup sugar
1/2 cup milk
1 teaspoon vanilla
1/4 teaspoon ground nutmeg
Sweetened whipped cream for
   topping, optional

Preheat oven to 350°. Spray a 15 x 10 x 1-inch baking pan with nonstick spray coating. In a medium mixing bowl, combine butter, sugar, salt, and egg yolk; stir to blend. Add flour. Stir until crumbly. Using milk, moisten as for pie crust. Form into ball. Pat into prepared baking pan, spreading evenly and forming a slight edge around all sides. Spread rhubarb and crushed pineapple over the surface. In a medium bowl, combine eggs, egg white, sugar, milk, and vanilla. Stir until well blended. Pour custard mixture over rhubarb and pineapple mixture. Sprinkle nutmeg over the surface. Bake for 45 minutes or until set and a knife inserted in center comes out clean. Serve warm with whipped cream, if desired. Makes about 10 to 12 servings.

Rhubarb Cake

An easy-to-make, moist cake that's sure to please the family.

Nonstick spray coating
1 1/2 cups packed brown sugar
1/2 cup butter or margarine, softened
1 egg
1/2 teaspoon salt
1 teaspoon baking soda
1 cup buttermilk or sour milk

1 teaspoon vanilla
2 cups all-purpose flour
1 1/2 cups finely cut rhubarb
1/4 cup granulated sugar, for topping
1 teaspoon ground cinnamon, for
   topping

Preheat oven to 375°. Spray a 13 x 9 x 2-inch baking pan with nonstick spray coating and lightly flour. In a large mixing bowl, cream brown sugar and butter until light. Beat in egg and salt. Dissolve baking soda in buttermilk. Stir in vanilla. Add to cream mixture alternately with flour, beginning and ending with flour. Stir in rhubarb, mixing only until well coated. Pour into prepared baking pan. In a small bowl, mix together granulated sugar and cinnamon; sprinkle over cake batter. Bake for about 40 to 45 minutes or until toothpick inserted in center comes out clean. Makes about 18 to 24 servings.

Rhubarb Crumble

Nonstick spray coating
1 cup packed brown sugar
3/4 cup rolled oats
1 cup all-purpose flour

1/3 cup butter, melted
1 teaspoon ground cinnamon
4 cups cut-up rhubarb

Preheat oven to 350°. Spray an 8 x 8-inch baking dish with nonstick spray coating. In a medium bowl, combine brown sugar, rolled oats, flour, butter, and cinnamon; stir until well blended. Arrange rhubarb in prepared baking dish. Sprinkle sugar mixture over rhubarb. Bake for 35 to 40 minutes or until rhubarb is tender and surface is lightly browned. Serve warm with cream or ice cream. Makes about 6 servings.

Rhubarb Ambrosia Betty

With a touch of orange and buttery bread, this dish makes a delightful Sunday dinner dessert.

Nonstick spray coating
4 cups cut-up rhubarb
1 1/2 cups sugar
I tablespoon all-purpose flour
1/4 teaspoon salt
1 orange, peeled and sections
    cubed

2 teaspoons grated orange peel,
    divided
4 cups cubed day-old bread, divided
1/2 cup butter or margarine, melted
    and divided
1/2 cup shredded coconut

Preheat oven to 350°. Spray an 8 x 8 x 2-inch baking dish with nonstick spray coating. In a large bowl, combine rhubarb, sugar, flour, salt, orange cubes, and 1 teaspoon orange peel; stir until well mixed. Add 2 cups bread cubes and 1/4 cup butter; mix well. Pour mixture into prepared baking dish. In a medium bowl, combine remaining orange peel, bread cubes, and butter with coconut; stir until well blended. Sprinkle over top of rhubarb mixture. Bake for about 40 minutes or until rhubarb is tender and top lightly browned*. Serve warm. Makes about 6 to 8 servings.

*Bake an additional 15 to 20 minutes or until rhubarb is tender if using frozen rhubarb.

School's Out Neighborhood Picnic

Recipes in This Chapter

As far as I was concerned, my mother was the best cook in the world. And the end of the school year, the Wide Awake School's picnic was the perfect opportunity to show off her cooking skills. When you're in first grade and the new kid in the local one-room school, you tend to get ideas like that.

The idea came to me when our teacher, Mrs. Larson, announced that the school board agreed to a picnic for the entire neighborhood on our final day.

"The school board will furnish the hot dogs, buns, and ice cream," she said. "And with a few other dishes, we will be able to have a nice picnic right here in our school."

Her words made me sit up straighter. Here was my mother's chance. As I listened to Mrs. Larson, I couldn't help wondering how Mom might feel about cooking for the whole neighborhood. As I pondered that thought I caught Mrs. Larson's next announcement.

"I have here some slips with suggestions on what each family can bring. I'm passing them out just so we don't end up with," she paused and looked around the room, "ten jars of beet pickles."

"BEET PICKLES," someone gasped. A general groan rolled around the room.

Betty Rose, the other first grader, turned around and wrinkled her nose. "Who likes beet pickles?"

I wrinkled my nose back. "Not me."

Across the aisle, Joey stuck his finger in his mouth and crossed his eyes. Betty Rose and I couldn't help giggling.

"Girls," Mrs. Larson warned. She went on explaining her picnic plans, but I wasn't really listening. I didn't know much about picnics. When we had our family picnics my mom furnished most of the food. Of course, my aunts helped . . . some.

I glanced around the room and did a quick count. There were thirteen kids in the entire eight grades and some were brothers and sisters. At most, I guessed we were lucky to have six maybe seven families. That didn't mean many dishes to pass. Mother could easily bring six more dishes all by herself.

"Where will we put all that food," a fifth-grade girl asked.

What did she mean all that food? Six dishes? That wasn't so much.

"We'll push my desk aside," Mrs. Larson explained, "and set up some planks on sawhorses. I have a pretty tablecloth that will be just right. After we eat, we'll have a short program to award diplomas to the graduating class. Following that, there will be games and contests outside. If anyone is still hungry, they can come in for more food."

More food? Six dishes and she expects leftovers?

Just when I dared to peek at the folded slip of paper Mrs. Larson handed me, Better Rose turned around.

"What's your mother bringing?"

"Cake," I whispered back. "Yours?"

"Egg salad sandwiches."

Great. Sandwiches and cake. Some picnic. Mrs. Larson needed to talk to my mother.

Just when I raised my hand, Mrs. Larson called on someone else. At that point, it occurred to me, I'd best talk to my mother first.

When I finally hinted at it to Mom, she only laughed and said, "Don't worry, there will be plenty to eat." I sighed. She just didn't understand. With only six other dishes for the entire neighborhood, how could there be enough to eat?

On the morning of the picnic, the first thing I noticed when I came down to breakfast was Mother's special red devil's food cake on the kitchen table. Next to it was a fancy bowl with orange and carrot gelatin. So far so good.

After looking over the counter and not seeing anything else, I just had to ask, "Is that all you're taking?"

Mother looked at me with a frown, "What do you mean, is that all I'm taking?"

"Well," I hesitated a bit, trying to find the right words. "I thought you'd take something more."

Mother's frown grew deeper.

"Well, it is the school picnic," I tried to point out, "for the entire neighborhood. There'll be a lot of people there."

Mother gave an exasperated sigh. "Well, I don't have anything else, unless you want me to take pickles."

I shrugged. "Pickles will be great." Mom was a great pickle maker and she had a whole lot of pickles on the shelf in the basement. Pickled crabapples. Pickled peaches. She even had some cute, little pickled pear tomatoes that tasted just like dill pickles. I just knew the kids would think they were neat. When she came up from the basement carrying a quart of the dreaded beet pickles of all things, I nearly died.

"Mom," I pleaded, "Nobody eats BEET PICKLES. Nobody!"

"Maybe not kids, but I bet the adults will," she said.

Mrs. Larson greeted us at the door and introduced Mother to the other ladies. Since I still wasn't convinced there'd be enough food to go around, I lingered a while just to check things out.

It was just as Mrs. Larson promised. A long tablecloth covered the ugly planks. You couldn't even see the sawhorses underneath.

Mrs. Larson took Mother's red devil's food cake and placed it on her desk next to three other cakes. Several mothers fussed over the table arranging dishes into some sort of order. Two women pushed aside an assortment of gelatin salads to make room for Mother's. It took three ladies to decide where to place the bowls of potato salad, before or after the three dishes of macaroni salad. Just when it looked like they'd reached a decision, another bowl appeared and the debate began again. I hadn't seen so much food since we had our last family picnic.

All the while Betty Rose's mother dished up our pickled beets, she kept exclaiming how pretty they looked, "They add just the right touch of bright color to the table." She sounded like she meant it.

Aside from my concerns about the picnic food, I don't remember much about my first picnic at Wide Awake School. I know we had games and several contests for both kids and adults, but I forgot who won what. I even forgot who graduated.

I do, however, remember how my mother and several other mothers wiped tears from their eyes when the eighth-grade boys lowered our school flag and we sang "God Bless America."

I also remember Mother handing me the empty beet pickle jar and turning to congratulate Mrs. Larson on planning a great picnic. "It was wonderful," she said. "I thought the table would collapse under all the food."

Mrs. Larson agreed. "If anyone went away hungry, it was their own fault."

As far as I could tell, the overloaded table hadn't surprised either one of them. But I still couldn't figure it out. Mrs. Larson had handed out only seven white slips of paper.

When we first walked in I counted, without Mother's beet pickles, at least sixteen different dishes. And that was before Joey's mother came in with a big crock of hot baked beans. The numbers just didn't add up.

I'd heard some talk at home about loaves and fishes in the Bible. Was there any connection?

When I brought the subject up on the way home, Mother laughed. "It's something like that," she explained. "Country folks always bring a little extra. It's the way we are."

Vi's Old-Time Macaroni Salad

This is a tasty picnic treat.

1 1/2 cups elbow macaroni
1 1/2 cups chopped celery
1/3 cup minced onion
6 thinly sliced radishes
2 tablespoons snipped parsley
1/2 cup minced dill pickles
3/4 cup grated processed sharp cheese

1 cup mayonnaise or salad dressing
2 tablespoons vinegar
2 teaspoons prepared mustard
1 teaspoon salt
1/8 teaspoon pepper
Snipped chives, for garnish
Paprika, for garnish

In a medium saucepan, cook macaroni in boiling, salted water until tender; drain and rinse. In a large mixing bowl, combine macaroni, celery, onion, radishes, parsley, pickles, and cheese; stir to blend. In a small mixing bowl, combine mayonnaise, vinegar, mustard, salt, and pepper; mix well. Pour into macaroni mixture and gently stir until well blended. Chill. Serve in a large bowl garnished with chives and a sprinkle of paprika, if desired. Makes about 6 to 8 servings.

Strawberry-Gelatin Cream Cheese Salad

Be sure to drain the crushed pineapple thoroughly. The pineapple juice is used as part of the liquid called for in the recipe.

2 3-ounce packages of strawberry-flavored gelatin
1 20-ounce can crushed pineapple, drained
Reserved pineapple juice

48 large marshmallows
3 tablespoons milk
4 ounces cream cheese, softened
1/2 cup chopped walnuts
Whipped cream for topping, optional

In a large bowl, follow package directions to make gelatin as usual, but use pineapple juice for part of the liquid. Do not refrigerate. In a saucepan, combine marshmallows and milk. Cook over medium heat, stirring constantly until melted. Add cream cheese and stir until completely dissolved. Remove from heat and add crushed pineapple and nuts; blend well. Stir into gelatin mixture until well mixed. Chill in refrigerator until set. Serve with a dollop of whipped cream, if desired. Makes about 6 to 8 servings.

Pork and Bean Salad
This is a great main-dish salad.

1 1-pound can pork and beans in
   tomato sauce
1/2 pound bologna, diced
1/2 pound sharp cheddar cheese,
   diced
1/2 cup finely chopped onion

1/3 cup sweet pickle relish
1/4 cup mayonnaise
1/8 teaspoon salt
1/8 teaspoon pepper
3 green pepper rings for garnish,
   optional

In a large mixing bowl, combine pork and beans, bologna, cheese, onion, pickle relish, mayonnaise, salt, and pepper. Toss gently but thoroughly. Refrigerate for at least 2 hours or overnight. Garnish with pepper rings, if desired. Makes about 5 to 6 servings.

Lou's Deviled Eggs
This is a tasty pairing of ham and dill pickle.

6 hard-boiled eggs, peeled
1/4 cup mayonnaise or salad dressing
2 tablespoons minced ham
2 tablespoons minced dill pickle
2 teaspoons minced onion

1/4 teaspoon salt
1/8 teaspoon pepper
1/8 teaspoon dry mustard
Black olive slices for garnish, optional

Halve eggs lengthwise and remove the yolks. Press yolks through a fine sieve or mash with a fork. In a small mixing bowl, combine yolks, mayonnaise, ham, dill pickle, onion, salt, pepper, and dry mustard; mix well. Fill egg white cavities with the mixture, using either a spoon or pastry tube. Top each egg with a slice of black olive, if desired. Chill. Serve arranged on an egg dish or a large platter. Makes 12 stuffed egg halves.

Prune Spice Cake

It's loaded with spicy, fruited flavors and is great to eat out of hand.

Nonstick spray coating
2 1/4 cups all-purpose flour
1 teaspoon baking soda
3/4 teaspoon baking powder
1 teaspoon ground cloves
1 teaspoon ground allspice
1 teaspoon ground cinnamon
3/4 teaspoon salt

1/2 cup shortening, softened
1 1/4 cups sugar
2 beaten eggs
1 cup cooked, chopped prunes
1 cup buttermilk or sour milk
Butter frosting (see recipe, below)
Chopped walnuts

Preheat oven to 375°. Spray a 13 x 9 x 2-inch baking pan with nonstick spray coating and lightly flour. In a medium bowl, combine flour, baking soda, baking powder, cloves, allspice, cinnamon, and salt. In a large mixing bowl, cream shortening. Gradually add sugar; cream together until light and fluffy. Add eggs, one at a time, beating well after each addition. Stir in prune pulp; mix well. Add flour mixture alternately with buttermilk, a small amount at a time, beating well. Pour batter into prepared pan. Bake for 40 to 45 minutes or until a toothpick inserted in center comes out clean. Cool on wire rack. When cake is cooled, frost with butter frosting and sprinkle walnuts over the top. Makes about 12 to 16 servings.

Creamy Butter Frosting

1/4 cup butter or margarine, softened
2 cups powdered sugar, divided
1 teaspoon vanilla
1/8 teaspoon salt
1-2 tablespoons cream, as needed

In a mixing bowl, beat butter until soft and creamy. Gradually add 1 cup powdered sugar, vanilla, and salt; beat until well mixed. Add remaining sugar alternately with cream, beating thoroughly after each addition. (Add only enough cream to make a smooth mixture suitable for spreading.) Makes about 2 cups enough to frost a 13 x 9 x 2-inch cake or 8- or 9-inch 2-layer cake.

Red Devil's Food Cake

I have no idea why Mother called this particular recipe red devil's food cake. I never saw a "red" chocolate cake. When I asked her about the cake's color and name, she admitted that the title also puzzled her. However, she guessed it got its name because it was so rich and tempting.

1/2 cup shortening, softened
1 3/4 cups sugar, divided
1 teaspoon salt
1 teaspoon vanilla
1 2/3 cups cold water, divided
1/2 cup cocoa

2 1/2 cups all-purpose flour
3 egg whites
1 1/2 teaspoons baking soda
Soft chocolate frosting (see recipe, page 68)

Preheat oven to 350°. Line two 8 x 8 x 2-inch baking pans with waxed paper. In a large mixing bowl, combine shortening and 1 cup sugar; cream together until light and fluffy. Beat in salt and vanilla. In a small bowl, combine 1/3 cup cold water and cocoa; stir until well blended. Beat into creamed mixture. Stir flour into creamed mixture alternately with 1 cup cold water, blending well after each addition. In a medium mixing bowl, beat egg whites with an electric mixer until soft peaks form. Gradually add remaining sugar, beating until stiff peaks form. Fold meringue into batter. In a small bowl, combine baking soda and remaining cold water; stir well to dissolve baking soda. Stir into batter, mixing thoroughly. Pour batter into prepared baking pans. Bake for 30 to 35 minutes or until toothpick inserted in center of cake comes out clean. Remove from oven and cool on wire racks. Remove waxed paper and frost middle and sides of cooled cake with soft chocolate frosting. Makes one 8-inch layer cake.

NOTE: At one time, cooks added red food coloring to their chocolate cake batter—in some cases up to 5 tablespoons. While this made for an eye-catching hue, the practice was discouraged when research reported a link between certain food dyes and cancer.

Soft Chocolate Frosting

1 cup sugar
3 tablespoons cornstarch
2 1-ounce squares unsweetened
    chocolate, grated

Dash of salt
1 cup boiling water
3 tablespoons butter
1 teaspoon vanilla

In a medium saucepan, combine sugar and cornstarch; stir to blend. Stir in chocolate and salt. Blend in water. Cook over medium-high heat, stirring constantly until the mixture thickens. Remove from heat. Stir in butter and vanilla. Spread on cake while hot for a glossy frosting that remains soft and smooth. Makes enough for an 8-inch 2-layer cake or a 13 x 9 x 2-inch cake.

SUMMER

Along a Country Road

So you're walking down a country road
Please, may I walk with you?
I love a country road
For I have mem'ries, too.

It was along a country road
My father walked with me,
'Twas here I learned from him
So much of nature's mystery.

Along a lovely lane like this I found
Sweet blood-root in the spring
And I learned the kinship I now share
With wild birds as they sing.

Soft evening sunsets, springtime's sweetness,
Warm summer's magic rare,
Rich autumn harvests, winter's bounty
All to be cherished there.

So if you're weary, stranger
Let me bear your load
And we'll walk a while and talk a while
And share this country road.

Anne M. Diley (1916–1969)

The Pleasures of Strawberries

Recipes in This Chapter

Happiness to most country cooks is a strawberry patch filled with clusters of crimson berries. At least it was to my mother. If she didn't find one already growing at our new farm location, she planted one at the first opportunity.

Back then it seemed that everyone had a family-size plot, so she had no problem finding plants. Strawberries are fairly easy to grow and with Mother's extraordinary green thumb, her plants flourished.

Once the season began, the sweet and juicy, plump and fragrant berries peeked out from their ground-hugging vines daring us to sample only one. Of course, we couldn't resist the strawberries —especially when sun-warmed and fresh-picked.

I remember the hours spent kneeling on straw mulch between rows. Morning after hot summer morning, I literally crawled on my knees down the paths. The summer breeze carried the distant meadowlark's song.

I'll confess to grumbling a bit in the early years about not having the handy quart containers I'd seen in the store. "How will we ever know how many quarts we've picked if all we have for picking is dish pans?" I asked.

Mother brushed my question aside. "Quart containers are not important. Berries taste the same in dishpans as they do in cute little boxes."

So I continued to pick the juicy berries and fill my large oval red and white dishpan, four, five, sometimes six, or more times.

Returning to the kitchen, I'd find Mother busy stemming berries and humming along to the music on the radio. She'd take one look at my strawberry-kissed lips and shake her head. "Guess you'll be too full for dessert at noon," she noted.

Of course, I wasn't.

Their fragrant aroma filled the kitchen throughout strawberry season. Mother always cooked up enough strawberry jam to last us all winter. The old chest freezer in the summer kitchen also held its share of berries. We ate our fill for breakfast, dinner, and supper. We enjoyed the mouth-watering berries, crushed or whole, with cream or milk on top of cereal, in fruit salads, on top of ice cream, in pies, shakes, and kuchens.

We relished old-fashioned strawberry shortcake more then any of the other dishes. In fact, it was my father's favorite dessert. Dad was a purist when it came to shortcake, insisting on only generous servings of berries and warm buttermilk biscuits.

"Strawberries ladled on angel food cake or sponge cake shells is not shortcake," he maintained. "It is only strawberries on cake. Neither is a skimpy mound of berries on a cold biscuit a proper shortcake." As we always had an abundance of sweetened crushed berries and Mother didn't mind baking biscuits, he was never disappointed.

I don't recall her ever measuring the berries for shortcake. She simply stirred in a sprinkle of sugar and left them on the kitchen counter to draw their juices. Since our cows produced rich milk and the cream rose daily to the top, Mother liberally whipped up bowls of heavenly sweetened clouds for topping. At dessert, we placed a large dish of berries in the middle of the table next to a platter of oven-fresh buttermilk biscuits. As I mentioned, Dad was never disappointed.

In late June, when the picking was almost finished, Mother looked to her sisters, neighbors, and friends for different ways to serve the gift of plenty from her patch. She tried some of their recipes once or twice. However, Dad always gave her his biggest smile when she announced, "Save some room for strawberry shortcake."

Crushed Strawberries with Buttermilk Biscuits

Of all the ways Mother served strawberries, shortcake rated No. 1. Sometimes she served whipped cream on top of the berries. Other times we enjoyed ice cream or plain sweetened berries over a warm biscuit.

5 cups sliced and/or crushed
    strawberries
1/2 cup sugar, or to taste
2 cups all-purpose flour
2 1/4 teaspoons baking powder
1/4 teaspoon baking soda

1 teaspoon salt
1/3 cup plus 2 teaspoons shortening
3/4 cup buttermilk
1 tablespoon melted butter for
    topping
Whipped cream

Preheat oven to 450°. In a large bowl, combine strawberries with sugar; mix well. Cover and let stand at room temperature at least 30 minutes or until juice flows freely. Meanwhile, mix biscuit dough. In a large bowl, combine flour, baking powder, baking soda, and salt. Cut in shortening with a pastry blender. Stir in buttermilk, mixing only until dry ingredients are moist. Turn out onto lightly floured surface. Roll out to 1/2- to 3/4-inch thickness. Cut with a 2-inch floured biscuit cutter and place on an ungreased cookie sheet. Brush tops with melted butter. Bake for 12 to 15 minutes or until evenly browned. To serve, split biscuits open while still warm and place on serving dishes. Spoon strawberries over biscuits and top with whipped cream. Makes about 5 to 6 generous servings.

Strawberry Custard Tart

This recipe calls for basic ingredients and is very easy to put together. It is the blend of fresh strawberries with custard that lends an old-fashioned flavor.

2 cups all-purpose flour	6 tablespoons cornstarch
2 tablespoons sugar	1/4 cup all-purpose flour
1/4 teaspoon salt	1/4 teaspoon salt
1/2 cup chilled butter	2 1/2 cups milk
3 tablespoons shortening	4 slightly beaten egg yolks
6 tablespoons water	1 tablespoon butter or margarine
Uncooked rice	2 teaspoons brandy
1 1/2 cups sliced strawberries	1 teaspoon vanilla
2 cups sugar, divided	6–8 cups whole strawberries

In a large mixing bowl, combine flour, 2 tablespoons sugar, and salt. With a pastry blender, cut in butter and shortening. Add water and stir with a fork to moisten. Form into a ball and turn onto a lightly floured board. Roll out to an 18 x 13-inch rectangle. Fit into a 15 x 10 x 1-inch baking pan. Make a rim and flute the edges. Chill. Preheat oven to 375°. Top pastry with waxed paper and fill baking pan with uncooked rice to keep dough from shrinking or puffing. Bake for 15 minutes. Remove rice and waxed paper. Bake for 10 minutes longer or until lightly browned. Cool.

In a medium saucepan, combine sliced strawberries and 1 cup sugar. Cook, stirring frequently, over medium heat for 15 minutes. Remove from heat and press through strainer. Let glaze cool. Makes 3/4 cup.

In a medium saucepan, combine the remaining sugar, cornstarch, flour, and salt; gradually blend in milk. Cook, stirring constantly, over low heat for about 10 minutes or until mixture thickens. Remove from heat and blend a little of hot mixture into egg yolks. Stir egg mixture into custard and continue to cook, stirring constantly, over low heat for 3 to 4 minutes. Remove from heat and stir in butter, brandy, and vanilla. Chill for 2 hours. Makes about 3 cups.

Just before serving, spread custard evenly over tart shell. Arrange whole strawberries in rows over custard. Spoon strawberry glaze over berries. Cut into 3-inch squares to serve. Makes about 15 servings.

Strawberry Angel Pie

Sample the pleasures of fresh berries, combined with strawberry gelatin chilled in a crisp meringue shell.

Nonstick spray coating
3 egg whites
1/4 teaspoon cream of tartar
Dash of salt
3/4 cup sugar
2 cups sliced fresh strawberries, sweetened to taste
Water

1 3-ounce package strawberry gelatin
1 tablespoon lemon juice
1 3-ounce package cream cheese, softened
Whipped cream, for garnish
6–8 whole strawberries, for garnish

Preheat oven to 275°. Spray a 9-inch pie plate with nonstick spray coating. In a large mixing bowl, beat egg whites, cream of tartar, and salt until stiff but not dry. Add sugar 1 tablespoon at a time and beat until stiff peaks form. Spread and shape into pie plate to form crust. Bake for 1 1/2 hours. Turn off oven and cool with door closed for 2 hours. Meanwhile, drain berries, reserving syrup; if needed, add water to make 1 cup. In a small saucepan, heat syrup to boiling. In a large mixing bowl, combine boiling syrup and gelatin; stir to dissolve. In a small bowl, stir lemon juice into softened cream cheese, then gradually beat into gelatin mixture. Continue beating until cream cheese is dissolved into the gelatin. Chill until partially set. Blend in strawberries. Spoon mixture into meringue shell. Chill well for several hours or overnight. To serve, garnish with whipped cream and whole strawberries. Makes one 9-inch pie, about 8 servings.

Strawberry Rhubarb Jam

No strawberries? That never stopped Mother from making this family favorite. The combination of fresh rhubarb and strawberry gelatin blended nicely to give us a great topping for pancakes, ice cream, or fresh homemade bread.

6 cups rhubarb, cut in 1-inch pieces
3 cups sugar
1 6-ounce package strawberry gelatin

In a large mixing bowl, combine rhubarb and sugar. Stir to completely coat rhubarb with sugar. Cover with foil. Let stand in refrigerator overnight. The following day, stir into a large kettle and bring to a low boil over medium-high heat. Cook, stirring occasionally with a wooden spoon, for 20 minutes. Remove from heat. Stir in gelatin and blend well. Pour into sterilized glass jars. Cover and store in refrigerator. Makes about 5 small jars.

Strawberry Coffee Cake

A tender, made-from-scratch coffee cake that will awaken fond memories. This basic recipe can be made with any ripe berries, or, if desired, chopped ripe peaches.

Nonstick spray coating
2 cups all-purpose flour
4 teaspoons baking powder
$1/3$ cup sugar
$3/4$ teaspoon salt
$1/3$ cup butter or margarine
$2/3$ cup milk

1 slightly beaten egg
$2 1/2$ cups sliced fresh strawberries
$1/4$ cup sugar, or to taste
$1/4$ cup butter or margarine
$1/4$ cup sugar
$1/3$ cup all-purpose flour

Preheat oven to 425°. Spray an 11 x 7 x 1 1/2-inch pan with nonstick spray coating. In a large mixing bowl, combine flour, baking powder, $1/3$ cup sugar, and salt. Cut in butter. In a small bowl, combine milk and egg, blending well. Stir into flour mixture, mixing only until moist. Spread into prepared pan. Spoon strawberries over the batter. Sprinkle with $1/4$ cup sugar. In a small bowl, combine $1/4$ cup butter, $1/4$ cup sugar, and $1/3$ cup flour; crumble over strawberries. Bake for 35 to 40 minutes or until a toothpick inserted in center comes out clean. Serve warm with ice cream, if desired. Makes about 8 servings.

Fresh Strawberry Salad

The delightful combination of fruit makes this a refreshing dish that can be used either as a salad or dessert. It also makes a great dish to carry to a church supper or potluck dinner.

Nonstick spray coating
1 6-ounce package strawberry
   gelatin
1 cup boiling water
3 cups sliced fresh strawberries,
   sweetened to taste

1 20-ounce can crushed pineapple,
   drained
3 medium bananas, mashed
1/4 teaspoon ground cinnamon
1/8 teaspoon ground nutmeg
1 8-ounce carton sour cream

Spray an 11 x 7 x 1 1/2-inch baking dish with nonstick spray coating. In a large bowl, combine gelatin and boiling water, stirring until gelatin is dissolved. Fold in strawberries with juice, pineapple, and bananas. Blend in cinnamon and nutmeg. Turn half of mixture into prepared baking dish. Refrigerate until firm, about 1 1/2 to 2 hours. Spread sour cream evenly over first layer. Carefully spoon rest of strawberry mixture over sour cream. Cover with foil and refrigerate overnight. Makes about 10 to 12 servings.

Strawberry Fool

This dessert, made from fresh strawberry purée and whipped cream, is light and creamy. Best of all, you can prepare and chill it 1 to 2 hours before serving.

2 cups fresh strawberries
2 tablespoons sugar, or to taste, divided
3/4 cup heavy cream
4 whole strawberries with stems, for garnish

In a medium bowl, slice strawberries. Sprinkle with 1 tablespoon sugar. Let stand 30 minutes or until juices are released. Drain berries through a fine strainer. Reserve pulp and juice separately. Purée the uncooked berries in a blender. In a medium mixing bowl, beat the cream until stiff. Gradually add remaining sugar. Fold strawberry pulp into cream just until mixture looks marbleized. Cover and chill. To serve, spoon into dessert dishes. Drizzle strawberry liquid over top. Garnish each with a whole strawberry. Makes 4 servings.

Strawberry Mellow

This is a light and luscious, easy-to-make dessert.

1 1/2 cups sliced strawberries
3 tablespoons sugar
1 teaspoon vanilla
2 cups whipped cream
1/2 pound miniature marshmallows

In a large bowl, combine strawberries and sugar. Cover and chill. Add vanilla to whipped cream and fold in marshmallows. Chill thoroughly. Before serving, fold cream mixture into strawberries. Makes about 6 servings.

The Ripening Garden

Recipes in This Chapter

If you happened to be looking for Mother anytime after she planted seeds in May and before the first autumn frost ended the growing season, you'd most likely find her in the garden. Flowers or vegetables, it made no difference.

She always had a bouquet of lush peonies, vivid zinnias, airy cosmos, or whatever might be blooming, somewhere in the house. Once they began ripening, she served fresh vegetables at every meal. Thinking back, I believe dill was her favorite garden herb. She planted a long row of it one year. After that, it reseeded itself and came up helter-skelter all over her garden. She didn't mind a bit. Being a resourceful person, she found a use for all of it.

Back in the Depression days Mother called her gravy with dill weed hard luck gravy. I was too young to know just what she was referring to, but it went over big in her country kitchen. The men ladled it generously over potatoes—boiled or mashed—and fresh baking powder biscuits. There was always another bowl waiting on her kitchen range. It certainly didn't seem like "hard luck" to me whenever she served it.

Times and luck changed and gradually we forgot about her gravy. Then, at a family gathering, we came around to talking about the old days and Mother's hard luck gravy. Everyone fondly recalled the poignant aromatic tang of dill grown in her garden.

"Shucks," Mother scoffed, "It was just a little fat browned with flour and dill, with milk added. We used dill in many ways in those days. It grew wild in the garden and the family liked the flavor.

"Remember," she recalled, "how in late summer we sliced fresh cucumbers, large onions, a green pepper, and fresh tomatoes together in a bowl? We added a tablespoon or more of minced dill to one cup of sour cream and poured it over the salad. We chilled it for at least an hour to blend the flavors."

Mother also used generous amounts of chopped dill with her buttered vegetables like carrots and beans. Dill, of course, played an important part in all her pickle making.

As in so many cases, old-time family favorites or necessity foods are today's gourmet dishes. I updated Mother's hard luck gravy recipe and tried it on my family and friends. They agreed it tasted great, but insisted I change the name to dill gravy and serve it often.

Dill Gravy

3 tablespoons butter
3 tablespoons flour
2 cups milk
$1/2$ cup sour cream
$3/4$ teaspoon salt

$1/8$ teaspoon pepper
$1/4$ cup snipped fresh dill weed or 2
   tablespoons dried dill weed
Salt, to taste
Pepper, to taste

In a large heavy skillet, melt butter over medium heat. Add flour and blend in with butter. Continue to stir to remove lumps and give the gravy a smooth texture. Slowly add the milk, stirring constantly; bring to boiling. Cook until smooth and thickened. Add the sour cream, but do not continue to cook. Season with salt and pepper. Add the dill weed and continue to stir until well blended. Serve warm. Makes about 2 $1/2$ cups.

NOTE: For best results, use fresh dill leaves. Cooking diminishes the flavor of fresh dill, so add just before serving.

Garden Fresh Peas and New Potatoes

Once the potatoes set their blossoms, Mother liked to carefully dig under the plants to, as she called it, "snitch" a few little ones to fix with just-picked peas. Little red potatoes are great served this way since they hold their shape. The more starchy Russets will do also. You just have to be careful not to overcook them.

24 walnut-sized new potatoes
3 cups fresh-picked and shelled peas
1 cup whole milk
4 tablespoons butter

1/4 cup snipped parsley
1 teaspoon salt
1/4 teaspoon pepper

Thoroughly wash and scrub new potatoes. Do not peel. In a medium saucepan, combine potatoes and peas in enough hot water to cover. Cover and cook over medium-high heat until potatoes are barely tender when pierced with a sharp fork, about 9 to 10 minutes. Drain. Lower heat. Return to heat. Add milk, butter, and parsley. Season to taste with salt and pepper. Simmer, stirring occasionally with a wooden spoon to avoid breaking up the potatoes, until the potatoes and peas are heated thoroughly. Do not overcook. Serve warm. Makes about 6 to 8 servings.

NOTE: Three cups of frozen peas may be substituted for fresh peas. If using frozen peas, follow cooking directions on package.

Yellow Bean 'n' Sour Cream Soup

Serve this soup piping hot with cold cuts or sandwiches for a light supper.

1 1/2 pounds yellow beans, trimmed
    and cut into 1-inch lengths
1/2 cup snipped parsley
1/2 teaspoon salt
6 strips of bacon, chopped
1 large onion, chopped

2 tablespoons all-purpose flour
1 tablespoon cider vinegar
1 cup sour cream
1/8 teaspoon pepper
Paprika for garnish, optional

In a large saucepan, cook beans, parsley, and salt in boiling water for 3 to 4 minutes or until beans are crisp-tender. Remove from heat. Drain, reserving liquid. In a large skillet, brown bacon over medium heat. Add the onion and sauté until crisp-tender. Stir in flour, blending well. Add vinegar and the liquid from the cooked bean mixture; stir to blend. Cook, stirring constantly, until smooth and creamy. Combine with bean mixture. Lower the heat and blend in sour cream and pepper. Cover and continue cooking for 2 minutes to thoroughly heat the mixture before serving. Do not boil. Serve warm with a dash of paprika, if desired. Makes about 4 to 6 servings.

Lettuce Salad and Parsley Dumplings

I have never been able to figure out why this combination was such a hit with our family, but it was. Just as soon as the leaf lettuce was ready in the garden, we looked forward to Mother making lettuce salad and parsley dumplings, just as her mother taught her. It is also a great pair to serve with roast beef or roast pork.

Lettuce Salad

10 cups of torn green leaf lettuce, washed and dried
6 green onions, chopped
Sweet mayonnaise dressing (see recipe below)

In a large salad bowl, toss together lettuce and onions. Chill. Just before serving, add the dressing and mix lightly. Makes about 4 to 6 servings.

Sweet Mayonnaise Dressing

1/2 cup mayonnaise or salad dressing
2 teaspoons sugar
4 teaspoons whole milk

In a small mixing bowl, combine mayonnaise, sugar, and milk. Whisk until smooth and thoroughly blended. Serve over lettuce salad. Makes about 1/2 cup.

Parsley Dumplings

2 cups all-purpose flour
2 eggs
$1/2$ cup milk
$1/2$ teaspoon salt
$1/2$ teaspoon baking powder

3 quarts water
1 tablespoon salt
2 tablespoons butter
3 tablespoons snipped parsley

In a medium mixing bowl, combine flour, eggs, milk, $1/2$ teaspoon salt, and baking powder. Beat with an electric mixer until light and bubbly. In a large kettle, bring water with 1 tablespoon of salt to boil over high heat. Drop dough into boiling water a teaspoonful at a time. Do not overcrowd. Do not stir while dumplings are cooking. As dumplings rise to the top, taste test for doneness. When done, remove one at a time using a slotted spoon, rinse lightly with cold water, and drain through a colander. In a medium saucepan, melt butter over medium heat; add drained dumplings and parsley. Cover the saucepan and shake backward and forward over the heat until dumplings are hot and coated with butter and parsley. Serve with lettuce salad. Makes about 4 to 6 servings.

Stewed Carrots and Cabbage

A simple but perfect pairing that is as tasty as it is attractive.

2 cups carrots, peeled and sliced in
  1/4-inch rounds
1 small head of cabbage, shredded
1 teaspoon salt, divided

2 tablespoons butter
1/8 teaspoon pepper
Snipped chives for garnish, optional

In separate saucepans, in enough lightly salted boiling water to cover, cook carrots and cabbage until barely tender, about 5 to 6 minutes. Drain. In a large saucepan, combine carrots and cabbage. Stir in butter. Season to taste with pepper and additional salt, if desired. Serve with a sprinkle of chives, if desired. Makes about 6 to 8 servings.

Country-Style Onions

Choose a medium-sized sweet onion for each serving or a large onion for two.

6 large sweet onions, peeled
1/2 teaspoon salt
2 tablespoons butter
4 strips of bacon, chopped

2 tablespoons cream
1 well-beaten egg
1/8 teaspoon pepper

Preheat oven to 350°. In a large saucepan, in enough lightly salted water to cover, cook onions over medium-high heat for 20 to 25 minutes until barely tender. Drain. In a baking pan that will comfortably hold the onions, melt the butter over medium heat. Brown onions in butter. Sprinkle bacon over onions. Place in oven and bake for 15 minutes. Remove from oven and let cool slightly. In a small bowl, combine cream and egg; blend well. Pour egg mixture over onions and bacon. Place baking pan back in oven and continue to bake until golden brown. Season to taste with pepper. Serve warm. Makes about 6 to 8 servings.

Cucumber, Onion, and Tomato Salad

This is one of those wonderful salads for which you can vary the size and amounts of the vegetables to suit your needs. If you wish, you can add some red and green peppers to the mix.

3 large cucumbers, peeled and thinly sliced	1 teaspoon sugar
1 large sweet onion, thinly sliced	1/4 teaspoon pepper
1 1/2 teaspoons salt	1 cup sour cream
3 tablespoons vinegar	2 medium tomatoes, cut into wedges
3 tablespoons water	Snipped fresh dill weed leaves for garnish, optional

In a large bowl, combine cucumbers and onion. Sprinkle with salt; lightly stir to blend. Set aside for 1 hour. Meanwhile, in a medium bowl, combine vinegar, water, sugar, and pepper; thoroughly blend. Fold in sour cream. Drain the cucumber-onion mixture. Add tomatoes. Pour the vinegar mixture over the vegetables. Lightly toss together until all vegetables are coated. Chill the salad for 1 to 2 hours. To serve, garnish with a sprinkle of fresh dill weed leaves, if desired. Makes about 6 to 8 servings.

Theresa's French Dressing

When the garden explodes with lettuce, tomatoes, cucumbers, radishes, and onions, it's time to serve fresh salads topped with this tasty homemade French dressing.

$1/2$ cup salad oil	1 tablespoon steak sauce
$1/3$ cup sugar	1 teaspoon salt
$1/3$ cup catsup	1 teaspoon sweet Hungarian paprika
$1/4$ cup white vinegar	1 small onion, grated

In a small bowl, combine salad oil, sugar, catsup, vinegar, steak sauce, salt, and paprika; mix well. Stir in onion. Beat with an electric mixer for 1 to 2 minutes or until thoroughly blended. Store in refrigerator. Shake well before using. Makes about 1 $3/4$ cups.

Helen's Salad Dressing

An old-fashioned sweet boiled dressing that's perfect over cucumbers or coleslaw.

$1/2$ cup sugar
$1/2$ cup white vinegar
2 teaspoons celery seed
$1/2$ teaspoon salt
2 tablespoons salad oil
2 tablespoons water

In a small saucepan, combine sugar, vinegar, celery seed, and salt. Bring to a boil over moderately high heat. Cook for 5 minutes. Cool. Pour into a pint jar. Add salad oil and water. Cover and shake well. Makes about 1 $1/4$ cups.

Paprika Beans and Tomatoes

An attractive dish everyone will like.

1 pound yellow beans	1/4 cup tomato sauce
1 1/2 tablespoons olive oil	Salt, to taste
4 green onions, chopped	Pepper, to taste
2 cloves garlic, or to taste, minced	Snipped parsley for garnish, optional
2 teaspoons sweet paprika	

Trim and wash beans; cut into 1-inch lengths. In a large saucepan, cook beans in boiling water, uncovered, about 5 minutes or until just tender. Drain. In a large skillet, heat oil over medium heat. Add onions and garlic; sauté for 1 minute. Blend in paprika. Stir in beans and tomato sauce; mix thoroughly with onion mixture. Cook over low heat until beans are heated through. Season with salt and pepper. Serve warm, garnished with a sprinkle of parsley, if desired. Makes 4 to 6 servings.

Stuffed Peppers

This is an easy dish to make on a busy day.

Nonstick spray coating
6 green peppers
1 teaspoon salt water
1 pound lean ground beef
1 large onion, chopped
1 cup cooked rice

1/2 cup bread crumbs
2 medium ripe tomatoes, chopped
1 teaspoon salt
1/4 teaspoon pepper
1/2 cup buttered bread crumbs*
1/2 cup water

Preheat oven to 350°. Spray a baking pan the size that peppers can stand upright in with nonstick spray coating. Wash green peppers and cut off tops. Let stand in salted water for about 1/2 hour. Drain upside down. In a large skillet, combine meat and onion. Cook over medium-high heat, stirring constantly, until meat is well browned and onion is tender. Add rice, bread crumbs, tomatoes, salt, and pepper; mix thoroughly. Fill peppers with meat mixture. Place in prepared baking pan. Cover with buttered bread crumbs. Add 1/2 cup water to bottom of pan. Bake for about 1 hour or until peppers test done. Serve warm. Makes about 5 to 6 servings.

*Buttered Bread Crumbs

Spread soft butter over day-old bread. Pull bread into crumbs with fork or use fingers to tear it into small pieces.

Fourth of July Family Picnics

Recipes in This Chapter

Next to Christmas, the Fourth of July, with its fireworks, flags, and special treats, was the most anticipated holiday of the year. And the Fourth of July was a natural time for family and friends to gather at our farm for a summer picnic. In fact, what started as a simple gathering when Dad was too busy haying and milking to go anywhere soon became an annual event.

Our Fourth celebration began early in the morning when Grandma brought out her two American flags and fastened them to the front porch. If anyone was proud to be an American, it was Grandma Wezmarovich. She considered it a patriotic duty to her adopted land to be the first in the neighborhood to display her flags.

Amidst "hi"s, hugs, and "How's everyone?" kids exploded from the first carloads and ran in all directions. The women with large wicker baskets of food followed Mother into our country kitchen. Hoisting a huge watermelon to his shoulder, Uncle Art headed for the pump house. A cousin from another car followed with a case of root beer to chill, along with the melon, in the water tank. The rattle and popping of firecrackers filled the air and continued until someone noticed Rover, our farm dog, quaking under the back steps.

"Enough of that," one aunt or the other, scolded.

"Shucks Mom, it's the Fourth of

July," a reluctant cousin protested, but the popping stopped. That is until his father started it all again.

The men, one by one, drifted out to the garden to help Dad select the season's first sweet corn. Once they brought in a full bushel basket, Mother engineered the husking. She liked to boil the young corn in their tender inner husks. That meant removing the outer husks, carefully pulling back the tender inner husks to remove the silks, and finally smoothing the inner husks back in place. Mother lined the bottom of her 20-quart canning kettle with a layer of discarded husks, arranged as many of the prepared cobs as possible, and covered them with more husks. After placing the kettle on the stove, she had the men fill it with cold well water. She left the covered kettle to boil.

"Why do you do you leave all those husks on?" I once asked.

"They add extra flavor to the young corn," she replied and turned her attention to helping her sisters arrange food on the extended kitchen table. Outside, the men were busy setting up card tables and chairs under the shady apple trees.

A bevy of kitchen helpers scurried about spreading their goodies on the tables and counter tops. I noticed several secretly tasting a dish or two in the process and even encouraging others to do the same.

Surrounding the platter of steaming corn sat two salt shakers and a dish with a whole pound of butter. An array of salads—everything from gelatin to potatoes, and relishes of fruits and vegetables—took up one end; baked beans, hot dogs and buns, and several hot casseroles waited at the other end.

In between sat plates of deviled eggs—sometimes we had four or five different versions. Every year each aunt brought a plate of eggs.

"Just to have a little extra," they explained. "They're so easy to make and so easy to carry, I just had to bring some."

They all assured one another you couldn't have too many deviled eggs.

Dad claimed it was a losing battle. In time, deviled eggs became as much of a Fourth of July tradition as the sound of popping firecrackers.

After searching, I found the desserts. A whole array of mouthwatering cakes, from angel food to chocolate, and peanut squares waited on the counter next to the coffee pot.

Once the weeping pitcher of chilled lemonade sat next to the sink, the women checked to see if everything planned for the table had made it to the table. Satisfied, they nodded to Mother to open the kitchen door and yell out, "Come and get it!"

All outside activity stopped and the rush toward the kitchen table began. Everyone paused just inside the crowded room for a short table blessing. Within seconds, the pushing and shoving nearly starved kids loaded their plates and headed back outdoors. The men lined up next to fill their plates. Once they went out the door, the women followed.

"There's more food inside. Help yourself to seconds," Mother announced before settling at a table beside her sisters. Some returned for second helpings, some even for thirds, and the food disappeared in short order.

Oh, and did I mention watermelon? That always came later, just when everyone claimed they couldn't eat one more bite. However, there's something about the sound of chilled and dripping wet watermelon snapping apart that captures one's attention and renews the appetite. Soon all the kids and a good share of the adults were wiping watermelon juice off their chins.

Once someone said "how about a card game," it didn't take long to clear the tables and put away the few leftovers. The younger generation began a softball game.

"Watch out for the windows," an aunt yelled out, but she was too late. The first home run hit shattered the chicken-house window, sending squawking hens into a sudden molt.

When the babies settled into their naps, the women sat around visiting and exchanging recipes, catching up on family happenings, community birthings and dyings. Some knitted. Some crocheted. All scolded the mischievous pranksters when the flashing barrage of firecrackers caused them to drop a stitch.

All too soon chore time rolled around and the picking up and gathering up began. As soon as the empty dishes were returned to the basket they came in and the weary kids were accounted for, the cars filled and began pulling out of the yard.

By the time the last car turned out of the driveway, Mom and Dad began their various evening chores. Grandma went around to the front of the house to carefully take down her flags.

I sat on the back steps comforting Rover and remembering how everyone said they they'd had a wonderful Fourth of July picnic. I guessed I had to agree with them.

Grandma D's Best Potato Salad

This is a slightly sweeter version of an old-fashioned family favorite.

1 cup mayonnaise or salad dressing
1 teaspoon prepared mustard
$1/2$ teaspoon celery seed
$1/2$ teaspoon salt
$1/8$ teaspoon pepper
4 large potatoes, boiled in jackets
    until tender, drained, cooled,
    peeled, cut into pieces

3 hard-boiled eggs
1 red bell pepper, cored and diced
6 green onions, diced
1 cup diced celery
$1/2$ cup sweet pickle relish
Dash of paprika for garnish, optional
Snipped parsley for garnish, optional

In a large bowl, combine mayonnaise, mustard, celery seed, salt, and pepper; mix well. Add potatoes, eggs, red bell pepper, onions, celery, and sweet pickle relish; mix lightly. Add additional mayonnaise, if desired. Cover. Chill. Serve garnished with paprika and a sprinkle of snipped parsley, if desired. Makes about 6 to 8 servings.

Ham and Kidney Bean Salad

This is an excellent salad to serve at a light meal.

1 16-ounce can kidney beans,
    drained (2 cups)
1 cup fully cooked ham, cut into $1/2$-
    inch pieces
$1/4$ cup mayonnaise or salad dressing
1 cup chopped celery
$1/3$ cup sweet pickle relish
2 tablespoons minced onion

$1/4$ teaspoon salt
Dash of pepper
$1 1/2$ teaspoons prepared mustard
$1/2$ teaspoon celery seed
$1/2$ teaspoon Worcestershire sauce
1 hard-boiled egg, sliced in rings for
    garnish, optional
Parsley for garnish, optional

In a large mixing bowl, combine kidney beans, ham, mayonnaise, celery, sweet pickle relish, onion, salt, pepper, mustard, celery seed, and Worcestershire sauce. Toss lightly. Chill several hours before serving. Serve in a large salad bowl. Overlap three egg rings in center of dish with a sprig of parsley on top for garnish, if desired. Makes about 6 to 8 servings.

Chicken Pineapple Salad

This one's a favorite at picnics.

1 1/2 cups cooked chicken, diced
1 cup celery, diced
1 8-ounce can pineapple chunks, diced and drained, reserving juice

1/2 cup sliced ripe olives
1 cup mayonnaise or salad dressing
Lettuce leaves for garnish, optional
Paprika for garnish, optional

In a medium mixing bowl, combine chicken, celery, pineapple, and black olives. Toss together lightly. Chill. In a small bowl, thin mayonnaise with a small amount of reserved pineapple juice. Before serving, blend mayonnaise mixture into chicken mixture. Serve in a bowl lined with lettuce leaves, if desired. Dust with a sprinkle of paprika, if desired. Makes about 6 to 8 servings.

Confetti Stuffed Eggs

Catsup lends an attractive color and interesting flavor to these deviled eggs.

6 hard-boiled eggs, peeled
1 tablespoon snipped chives
3/4 teaspoon barbecue spice
2 tablespoons finely chopped pimiento

1 tablespoon catsup
1 1/2 teaspoons vinegar
Cherry tomato slices for garnish, optional

Halve eggs lengthwise and remove yolks. Press yolks through a fine sieve or mash with a folk. In a small mixing bowl, combine yolks, chives, barbecue spice, pimiento, catsup, and vinegar; mix well. Fill egg white cavities with the mixture, using either a spoon or pastry tube. Place a single cherry tomato slice on each yolk mixture, if desired. Chill. Serve arranged on an egg dish or a large platter. Makes 12 stuffed egg halves.

Rose's Deviled Eggs

The minced carrots lend a hint of color and crunch, and the mustard adds the nippy flavor.

6 hard-boiled eggs, peeled	1 tablespoon horseradish mustard
1/3 cup minced carrots	1 teaspoon lemon juice
2 tablespoons mayonnaise or salad dressing	1/8 teaspoon salt
1 tablespoon minced celery	Snipped parsley for garnish, optional

Halve eggs lengthwise and remove yolks. Press yolks through a fine sieve or mash with a fork. In a small mixing bowl, combine yolks, carrots, mayonnaise, celery, mustard, lemon juice, and salt; mix well. Fill egg white cavities with the mixture, using either a spoon or a pastry tube. Sprinkle each deviled egg with parsley, if desired. Chill. Serve arranged on an egg dish or a large platter. Makes 12 stuffed egg halves.

Peanut Cakes

This makes a great picnic treat for peanut-loving kids of all ages.

Nonstick spray coating
3 cups all-purpose flour
2 teaspoons baking powder, divided
1/4 teaspoon salt
2/3 cup shortening
1 1/2 cups sugar

1 teaspoon vanilla
1 cup water
4 egg whites, beaten stiffly
Powdered sugar frosting (see recipe, page 23)
1 1/2 cups ground salted peanuts

Preheat oven to 350°. Spray a 13 x 9 x 2-inch baking pan with nonstick spray coating and lightly flour. In a medium bowl, combine flour, 1 teaspoon baking powder, and salt. In a large mixing bowl, cream together shortening, sugar, and vanilla. Add flour mixture alternately with water, beginning and ending with flour, beating well after each addition. Fold in egg whites beaten with remaining baking powder. Pour batter into prepared baking pan. Bake for 30 to 35 minutes or until toothpick inserted in center comes out clean. Cool. Cut cake into small squares. Frost on all sides with powdered sugar frosting and then roll in peanuts. Makes about 36 servings.

Feeding the Threshers

Recipes in This Chapter

Nine was a good age to be when the threshing crew came to our farm. I don't know why I remember that year so well. Maybe it was because I could still be a tomboy, running, hiding, playing, driving a team with Father's help, and at the same time be too young to help in the kitchen.

Back in those days, the farm homes had sizeable dining rooms that allowed Mother to stretch out her table with 12 leaves as far as it could reach. Just like all of her neighbors, Mother filled the table with every special dish she could make.

The competition between Mother and her friends to set the best table was quite keen. I won't say they tried to outdo one another, but each gave the hungry men a feast fit for a king. Naturally, the men were not above doing a little comparing and teasing to help the situation.

The threshing crew usually arrived when Mother's ample garden was at its peak, so vegetables were not a problem. Neither were the meat and dairy products. Fresh spring chickens were in good supply, too. She often fixed 11 to 12 heavy spring fryers for a noon meal. Keeping ahead of the everlasting demand for homemade bread and desserts kept her in the kitchen for long hours. Meal plans usually included two or three different pies for the noon meal and two different cakes for supper. She served cookies for the snacks. And everything was baked fresh daily in a wood-stove oven without a thermostat. She enjoyed the challenge of preparing three square meals and two mid-meal snacks for 20 to 25 hungry men.

Serving these meals usually lasted three or four days depending on the grain acreage and the weather conditions. Sometimes the frantic pace in the kitchen lasted a week or two if we hit a rainy spell.

Each morning I helped Mother dig a pail of fresh new potatoes with skins so tender we only needed to brush them clean under running water. New carrots, tender and long, didn't get peeled either. Mother fixed them with butter and large onions that had the men asking for three and four helpings. Fresh-cut green and red cabbage always made a good salad. Naturally, she made her own salad dressing.

I recall certain young men on the threshing crew needed to be watched each year. They came to the table late, passed up the meat, potatoes, and vegetables, and helped themselves to three and four wedges of several kinds of pie.

"Oh, no you don't," Mother said one time, reaching right in and taking a pie plate out of a surprised boy's hand. "You start right here and now," she told him, placing a potato dish in his hands. He did, too.

Perhaps the best time of the meal was when the men left the table and the cooks cleared a place for themselves. We lingered over dessert, talking about neighborhood things, the babies being born, the marriages and the deaths. Just the women talked. I could sit and listen, but Mother didn't hold with my joining the conversation.

When I was nine, some kind person generally sent me outside to look around at dish washing time. "Too many people in the way as it is," she said. So I went out to see if Dad needed help driving horses or leveling off the oats so they didn't pile up in the corner of the grain bin.

I guess what I marvel at most now, as I look back on those days, is the fact that Mother and her friends did this tremendous amount of cooking in the old-fashioned country kitchen without ample refrigeration and the handy electric appliances I enjoy using today. Times have changed in country kitchens. While Mother was up at dawn to start her baking before the day's heat set in, I simply rely on my refrigerator and freezer to chill my salads and pies. I bake ahead and freeze. Mother and the old wood range were constant companions. Which makes me wonder: Were the good old days so good?

Swiss Steak

This is an old-fashioned country kitchen recipe considered by my grandmother and mother to be the very best way to prepare round steak, a cut that needs tenderizing.

1 1/2–2 pounds boneless round steak	1 cup chopped onion
1/2 cup all-purpose flour	2 cups chopped fresh tomatoes*
1 teaspoon salt	Water, as needed
1/4 teaspoon pepper	
2 tablespoons shortening, or as needed	

Trim excess fat from steak and cut into serving-size pieces. Mix flour with salt and pepper. Sprinkle flour mixture evenly on both sides of steak. Place meat on a large sheet of waxed paper; pound with a meat mallet or the side of a heavy plate. In a large heavy skillet or Dutch oven, melt shortening over medium-high heat. Brown steak evenly on both sides. Add onions when you first turn the steak. Lower the heat. Scrape up any brown bits on the bottom of the skillet and stir in. Add tomatoes. Cover and simmer about 1 to 1 1/2 hours or until steak is fork-tender, adding water if necessary. Makes about 4 to 6 servings.

*Stewed tomatoes may be used instead of fresh tomatoes.

Hungarian Beef Goulash

Ten different Hungarian cooks will give you ten different goulash recipes. This was my mother's version as taught to her by my grandmother. Popular with harvesting crews, this also makes a wonderful one-dish meal when served with dill pickles, fresh homemade bread, and plenty of good coffee.

3 tablespoons bacon drippings
3 pounds beef (chuck or rump), cut into 2-inch pieces
4 medium onions, coarsely chopped
3 rounded tablespoons sweet paprika
1 cup water, or enough to cover ingredients

1 medium green pepper, cored, seeded and cut into 4 pieces
1 1/2 teaspoons salt
1/4 teaspoon pepper
5 medium potatoes, peeled and quartered

In a Dutch oven or large skillet, heat bacon fat over medium-high heat, browning a few pieces of beef at a time until well browned on all sides. Remove beef and add onions. Cook 2 to 3 minutes or until onions are limp. Return beef to the Dutch oven. Add paprika, stirring to coat the meat evenly. Add water, green pepper, salt, and pepper. Cover and cook over very low heat for 1 1/2 to 2 hours or until meat is tender when pierced with a fork. Add potatoes and enough water to cover them. Cook another 1/2 hour or until potatoes are done. Taste to adjust seasonings. Serve piping hot. Makes about 6 to 8 servings.

Caraway Green Beans

The combination of caraway seed with the cheeses makes this a special dish to serve company.

2 pounds fresh green beans
2 tablespoons all-purpose flour
1/2 cup sour cream
2 tablespoons minced onion
1 tablespoon sugar
1/2 teaspoon salt
Dash pepper

3/4 cup milk
4 ounces caraway cheddar cheese, diced in 1/4-inch cubes
2 tablespoons grated Parmesan cheese
Strips of sweet red pepper for garnish, optional

Wash and trim beans; cut into 2-inch lengths. In a medium saucepan, cook beans in boiling water for 5 to 6 minutes or until just tender when pierced with a fork. Drain. In a medium saucepan over medium heat, blend flour, sour cream, onion, sugar, salt, and pepper. Gradually stir in milk, stirring until thickened and smooth. Add caraway cheddar and Parmesan cheeses and stir until melted. Stir in beans. Continue to cook over medium-low heat until beans are thoroughly heated, stirring occasionally. Serve warm with several strips of sweet red peppers for garnish, if desired. Makes about 6 to 8 servings.

Dilly Carrots

The addition of fresh snipped dill makes this a very tasty vegetable dish.

2 pounds carrots, trimmed and sliced diagonally, 1/2-inch thick (about 4 1/2 cups)
Water, as needed
4 tablespoons butter or margarine

1 teaspoon Dijon-style mustard
1 teaspoon seasoned salt
Dash pepper
3 tablespoons chopped fresh dill, plus additional for garnish

In a large saucepan, combine carrots with enough water to cover. Cover saucepan. Bring carrots to a boil over high heat. Lower heat and simmer carrots for 8 to 10 minutes or until just tender. Drain thoroughly. Stir in butter, mustard, salt, and pepper; mix well. Stir in fresh dill. Simmer, tossing until butter is melted and carrots are well coated, for 2 to 3 minutes longer. Serve very hot, garnished with additional dill, if desired. Makes about 5 to 6 servings.

German Red Cabbage with Apples

This is a colorful side dish to serve with either beef or pork.

1 head (1 pound) red cabbage, shredded
1/2 teaspoon salt
1/4 teaspoon pepper
3 tart red apples, cored and thinly sliced
3 tablespoons bacon drippings

1 medium onion, chopped
1/4 cup red wine vinegar
1/4 cup brown sugar
1 small bay leaf
1/2 teaspoon caraway seeds
Water, as needed

In a large bowl, combine cabbage, salt, and pepper. Add apples and stir to blend. In a large skillet over medium heat, melt bacon drippings and sauté onion until limp. Add cabbage mixture. Simmer until moisture is absorbed. Add vinegar, sugar, bay leaf, and caraway seeds. Reduce heat, cover, and simmer until cabbage is tender and liquid reduced, about 15 to 20 minutes, adding water as needed to prevent the cabbage from sticking. Remove bay leaf. Serve immediately. Makes about 6 to 8 servings.

Lyonnaise Potatoes

Unless you have a very large skillet, consider sautéing the potatoes in two batches, adding more shortening as needed to maintain an even browning on both sides.

3 tablespoons shortening, or as needed
4 cups thinly sliced cooked potatoes
1 medium onion, thinly sliced

1 teaspoon salt
1/4 teaspoon pepper
Snipped parsley for garnish, optional

In a large skillet over medium-low heat, heat shortening. Add potatoes and onion. Spread out in a thin layer. Add salt and pepper. Cook, stirring often until potatoes are golden brown on both sides. Continue to heat for 1 minute longer. Serve at once with a sprinkling of parsley, if desired. Makes 4 to 6 servings.

Creamy Coleslaw

The green and red peppers lend a touch of color and flavor to this simple salad.

1 cup sour cream
1/4 cup cider vinegar
1/4 cup sugar
1 teaspoon salt
1/4 teaspoon pepper

1 quart shredded crisp cabbage
1/4 cup minced green pepper
1/4 cup minced sweet red pepper
Dash of paprika for garnish, optional

In a small bowl, combine sour cream, vinegar, sugar, salt, and pepper; mix well. In a large bowl, combine cabbage, green and red peppers, and sour cream mixture. Toss gently until cabbage is well coated. Serve with paprika for garnish, if desired. Makes 4 to 6 servings.

Alice's No-Knead Bread Rolls

Even on a busy day it's easy to bake these small rolls.

Nonstick spray coating
1 package dry yeast
1/4 cup lukewarm water
1/4 cup shortening
2 tablespoons sugar

1 1/4 teaspoons salt
1 cup boiling water
1 beaten egg
3 1/2–4 cups all-purpose flour
Melted butter for topping, as needed

Spray a large bowl with nonstick spray coating. In a small bowl, combine yeast and lukewarm water. In a large mixing bowl, combine shortening, sugar, and salt. Add boiling water; stir until ingredients are dissolved. Cool to lukewarm. Add yeast and egg; stir until well mixed. Stir in 3 cups flour. Add more flour as needed to make a soft dough. Place dough in prepared bowl. Cover. Chill dough 2 to 24 hours. Meanwhile, spray 2 muffin tins with nonstick spray coating. Pinch off pieces of chilled dough large enough to fill muffin cups 1/2 full. Brush tops with melted butter. Cover and let rise until doubled, about 2 hours. Preheat oven to 425°. Bake 15 to 20 minutes or until nicely browned. Makes about 18 to 20 rolls.

Sweet and Sour Bean Combo
In place of fresh beans, canned or frozen may be used.

2 cups cooked green beans
2 cups cooked yellow beans
2 cups cooked peas
2 tablespoons butter
1 medium onion, chopped
2 tablespoons cornstarch
1 1/4 cups cooking liquid from beans
   and peas

1/3 cup cider vinegar
1 tablespoon brown sugar
1 teaspoon salt
1/8 teaspoon pepper
1 cup drained kidney beans
1 tablespoon snipped parsley for
   garnish, optional

Trim and snip green and yellow beans into 2-inch pieces. Cook beans in boiling water for 8 to 10 minutes or until crisp-tender. Drain, reserving liquid. Place shelled peas in just enough boiling water to cover. Simmer 8 to 10 minutes depending on the size of the peas. Drain, reserving liquid. In a large skillet, melt butter and sauté onion until tender. Stir in cornstarch. Gradually stir in cooking liquid and vinegar until smooth. Add sugar, salt, and pepper. Stirring constantly, bring to a boil and cook 1 minute. Add green beans, yellow beans, and kidney beans; heat thoroughly. Serve warm with a sprinkling of parsley, if desired. Makes 6 to 8 servings.

Grandma Doughty's Boiled Spice Cake

This is a heavy, moist cake. You can either serve it with your favorite powdered sugar icing or as Mother sometimes did. As soon as the cake came out of the oven, she lightly spread butter over it and then sprinkled it with granulated sugar. Delicious!

2 cups sugar
2 cups water
2 cups raisins
1 cup lard
2 teaspoons ground cloves

2 teaspoons ground cinnamon
1 teaspoon salt
3 cups all-purpose flour
2 teaspoons baking soda
Nonstick spray coating

In a large saucepan, combine sugar, water, raisins, lard, cloves, cinnamon, and salt. Bring to a boil over medium-high heat and cook for 4 to 5 minutes or until ingredients are well mixed and lard is melted. Remove from heat and cool. Meanwhile, preheat oven to 350°. Spray a 13 x 9 x 2-inch baking pan with nonstick spray coating. When boiled mixture has cooled, stir in flour and baking soda. Pour batter into prepared pan. Bake for 40 to 45 minutes or until toothpick inserted in center comes out clean. Cool. Serve plain or frosted with your favorite powdered sugar icing. Makes about 12 to 15 servings.

Mom's Cherry Pie

This cherry pie recipe is our family's favorite for as long as I can remember. I relied on it for 4-H and high school cooking demonstrations—and as an after-date snack for my future husband.

Flaky pastry for a double-crust pie
   (see recipe, page 56)
4 cups pitted tart cherries
3 tablespoons quick-cooking tapioca
1 1/2 cups sugar

1/4 teaspoon almond extract
1 tablespoon butter
Milk for crust topping, optional
Sugar for crust topping, optional

In a large bowl, combine cherries, tapioca, sugar, and almond extract. Mix well. Let stand for 15 minutes, stirring occasionally. Meanwhile, preheat oven to 400°. Line a 9-inch pie pan with pastry. Fill pastry with cherry mixture. Dot cherries with butter. Top with layer of pastry. Seal and flute with fork or fingers. Cut several slits in crust. Lightly brush milk over crust, if desired. Sprinkle sugar over milk, if desired. Bake for 45 to 50 minutes or until crust is nicely browned and filling gently bubbles to the surface. Cool on wire rack. Serve warm or cold with vanilla ice cream or sweetened whipped cream. Makes one 9-inch pie.

Raspberry Sour Cream Pie

Crowned with whipped cream, this pie is simply luscious.

1 unbaked 9-inch single-crust pie shell
    with high rim (see recipe, page 37)
12 ounces cream cheese, softened
1 cup sugar, divided
2 lightly beaten eggs
1 cup sour cream
5 tablespoons cornstarch
2 10-ounce packages frozen
    raspberries, thawed
1 cup heavy whipping cream,
    whipped
Sweetened whipped cream for
    garnish, optional
Whole raspberries for garnish,
    optional

Preheat oven to 375°. In a medium mixing bowl, beat together cream cheese, $1/2$ cup sugar, and eggs until smooth. Pour into pie shell. Bake for 30 minutes or until filling sets. Remove from oven and cool on wire rack. Spread sour cream evenly over top and chill for 1 hour. In a heavy saucepan, combine remaining sugar and cornstarch. Add berries. Mix well. Cook over low heat, stirring often, until mixture is thick and clear. Remove from heat. Cool to room temperature. Fold heavy whipping cream into cooled raspberry mixture. Spoon over top of pie. Chill several hours or overnight. Garnish with sweetened whipped cream and whole berries, if desired. Makes one 9-inch pie, about 6 to 8 servings.

The Love Apples of August

Recipes in This Chapter

Along about the middle of August, if you dropped in at most any country kitchen for a visit you'd find an irresistible aroma floating in the air: tomatoes! From the first red tomato until frost, garden-fresh, sun-ripened tomatoes were a versatile staple at most every meal.

Tomato season is a time to let the imagination run wild, looking for tantalizing ways to serve them. But no matter how much Mother tried to come up with new tomato recipes, the simplest old-fashioned ones pleased her family the most.

There is nothing quite like tomatoes and onions layered between two mayonnaise-coated slices of fresh homemade bread. Still warm from the summer sun, slices of red and yellow tomatoes looked palate-pleasing and pretty arranged on a large platter. Dad liked his served with a sprinkling of sugar. I preferred mine with a dash of salt. The hired man added a splash of vinegar to his.

It all started in winter, when Mother first sat down to dream over her seed catalog. More than once I heard her pledge, "We are not going to plant so many tomatoes this spring. We had far too many last summer. We don't really need two dozen tomato plants. We really should cut back, but what if we have an off year?"

When planting time came, she never did cut back. She never had a tomato crop failure either. Every year the prolific plants produced big red juicy tomatoes. Bushels and bushels of them—so many that Mother couldn't keep up. We gave away a good share to gardenless relatives, friends, neighbors, and anyone who happened to drive in the yard.

Dad never mentioned Mother's pledge to cut down. He enjoyed his early morning visits to the tomato patch seeking out the first ripe tomato hiding under the vines. When he brought it in and we all admired it, he went back to look for more. And he found them.

Dad never made a comment; he simply kept picking. Sometimes three, four, or even five bushels of ready-to-burst tomatoes sat on the back porch waiting for Mother's attention. When she looked at them and sighed, Dad only grinned and wisely said nothing. He knew that Mother enjoyed tomatoes. Once she saw the dark red vine-ripened tomatoes she caught "tomato canning fever." Big jars, little jars, fat and skinny jars—she'd fill anything that held a seal with tomatoes!

Granted, she did have a goal in mind that included 100 quarts of stewed tomatoes and another 100 quarts of juice. Most years she surpassed her goal—and used the rest for sauce, catsup, relish, pickles, and tomato jam.

It took a lot of hard work and long hours over steaming canning kettles for Mother to fill all those jars. However, she never complained. Every fall her basement shelves gleamed with brilliant jars of "put-up" tomatoes. Best of all, she found a use for them in everything from soups, stews, casseroles, salads, sauces, pasta, preserves, and pickles to main and side dishes and even some breads and desserts.

By the time the seed catalogs arrived the following winter, the basement shelves held only empty jars. Mother was already planning her next summer's garden.

Tomato Salad with Green Pepper

Red tomatoes paired with green peppers make a tasty and eye-catching combination—a country kitchen favorite.

1/4 cup cider vinegar	5 medium tomatoes
1/4 cup salad oil	1/2 cup diced green pepper
2 tablespoons sugar	1/2 cup diced onion
1/4 teaspoon salt	2 tablespoons snipped parsley
1/8 teaspoon pepper	

In a screw-top jar, combine vinegar, salad oil, sugar, salt, and pepper. Cover jar tightly and chill in refrigerator. Wash and peel tomatoes. Chill thoroughly in refrigerator. When ready to serve, cut tomatoes into small pieces. In a medium salad bowl, combine tomatoes, green pepper, onion, and parsley. Stir gently to mix. Vigorously shake jar of dressing to thoroughly blend. Pour over salad. Toss lightly to mix. Serve immediately. Makes 5 to 6 servings.

Cream of Tomato Soup

This is an old-fashioned, family-pleasing soup that is quick and easy to prepare with tomato juice.

5 cups tomato juice	1 teaspoon salt
1/4 teaspoon baking soda	1/8 teaspoon pepper
4 tablespoons butter	2 cups milk
4 tablespoons all-purpose flour	2 teaspoons lemon juice

In a small saucepan over medium heat, bring tomato juice to gentle boil. Add baking soda, stirring fast to keep it from boiling over. Remove from heat. In a medium saucepan over medium heat, melt butter. Blend in flour, salt, and pepper. Gradually add milk. Cook, stirring constantly, until thickened and smooth. Cook for 1 to 2 minutes longer. Lower heat. Stir in hot tomato juice and lemon juice. Mix well. Continue cooking for 4 to 5 minutes more to blend flavors. Serve hot with crackers or toast. Makes 5 to 6 servings.

Yellow Tomato Soup

This lovely golden, light soup is packed with flavor.

2 cups peeled and chopped yellow
   tomatoes
4 cups water
1 medium onion, minced
1/2 cup chopped celery with leaves
1 medium bay leaf
2 cups milk

2 tablespoons butter
1/2 teaspoon salt
1/4 teaspoon pepper
1/4 teaspoon baking soda
2 tablespoons snipped parsley
4 cups oyster crackers
1/2 teaspoon paprika, optional

In a large saucepan, combine tomatoes, water, onion, celery, and bay leaf. Cover and cook over medium-high heat for 15 to 20 minutes or until vegetables are tender. Add milk, butter, salt, and pepper. Stir to blend. Bring mixture to gentle boil. Stir in baking soda, stirring fast to keep it from boiling over. Lower heat and simmer 10 to 15 minutes for flavors to blend. Stir in parsley. Divide oyster crackers between soup bowls. Pour hot soup over crackers. Sprinkle with a dash of paprika, if desired. Makes 4 to 5 servings.

Cheesy Rice-Stuffed Tomatoes

Stuffed tomatoes can be prepared ahead and baked before serving.

Nonstick spray coating
6 large, firm red tomatoes
Salt, as needed
3 tablespoons butter
1 medium green pepper, chopped
1 medium onion, chopped
1 clove garlic, minced
1/4 cup shredded sharp cheddar
	cheese
1 cup cooked long-grain rice

1 beaten egg
1/2 teaspoon salt
1/8 teaspoon pepper
4 slices bacon, cooked and
	crumbled
3 tablespoons crushed cracker
	crumbs
6 teaspoons butter
Snipped parsley for garnish, optional

Preheat oven to 350°. Spray an 11 x 7 x 2-inch baking pan with nonstick spray coating. Wash tomatoes and cut a slice from the top of each. Using a sharp-edged spoon, scoop out the pulp, leaving the shell intact and reserving pulp. Sprinkle the inside of tomato shells lightly with salt. Invert each on rack to drain. Chop the pulp into bite-sized pieces. In a large skillet, melt butter over medium heat; sauté green pepper, onion, and garlic until all are tender but not browned. Remove from heat. Add the tomato pulp, cheese, rice, egg, 1/2 teaspoon salt, pepper, and bacon. Mix well. Spoon the mixture into tomato shells and place in prepared baking pan. Sprinkle each with cracker crumbs and dot with 1 teaspoon of butter. Bake for 30 to 35 minutes or until tomato mixture is heated through. Serve hot, garnished with a sprinkle of parsley, if desired. Makes 6 servings.

Tomato, Green Pepper, and Zucchini Sauté

Garden-fresh vegetables make this a light and tasty summer side dish.

3 tablespoons butter or margarine
1 large green pepper, seeded and
   cut into strips
1 large onion, sliced
1 clove garlic, minced
4–5 cups zucchini, cut into 1-inch
   cubes

5 large tomatoes, peeled and cut
   into wedges
1 teaspoon salt
1/8 teaspoon pepper
1 tablespoon snipped parsley for
   garnish, optional

In a large skillet, heat butter over medium-high heat. Sauté green pepper, onion, and garlic until onion is golden. Add zucchini, tomatoes, salt, and pepper. Lower heat. Cover. Simmer for 20 to 25 minutes or until vegetables are tender. Serve hot with a sprinkle of parsley, if desired. Makes 6 to 8 servings.

Scalloped Tomatoes

This tasty old-fashioned dish goes well with roast beef, pork, or fried chicken.

Nonstick spray coating
3 tablespoons butter
1 medium onion, chopped
3 cups crumbs made from day-old
   bread
6 medium red tomatoes, peeled and
   sliced in 1/2-inch slices

2 teaspoons sugar, divided
3/4 teaspoon salt, divided
1/4 teaspoon pepper, divided
1 tablespoon snipped chives for
   garnish, optional

Preheat oven to 350°. Lightly spray a 2-quart casserole with nonstick spray coating. In a medium saucepan over medium-high heat, melt butter. Add onion and cook, stirring often, until tender. Stir in crumbs. In prepared casserole, layer 1/3 of the tomatoes on bottom. Sprinkle with 1 teaspoon sugar, 1/2 the salt, and 1/2 the pepper. Top with 1/3 of the onion/crumb mixture. Repeat layers two more times, ending with the remaining onion/crumb mixture on top. Sprinkle snipped chives over all, if desired. Bake uncovered for 1 hour or until tomatoes are bubbling and crumbs are a golden brown. Serve hot. Makes about 6 to 8 servings.

Texas Tomato Hash

This is a great baked dish to serve on a busy day.

Nonstick spray coating
2 tablespoons butter or margarine
3 medium onions, chopped
1 large green pepper, minced
1 pound ground beef
2 cups cooked tomatoes

$1/2$ cup uncooked long-grain rice
1 tablespoon chili powder
1 $1/2$ teaspoons salt
$1/8$ teaspoon pepper
3 green pepper rings for garnish,
    optional

Preheat oven to 350°. Lightly spray a 2-quart ovenproof casserole with nonstick spray coating. In a large saucepan over medium heat, add butter and sauté onions and green pepper until onions are limp and yellow. Add the ground beef. Cook until meat is browned. Stir in tomatoes, rice, chili powder, salt, and pepper. Mix well. Pour into prepared casserole. Cover and bake for 1 hour. Remove cover and continue baking for 15 minutes longer to allow top to brown. Serve hot, garnished with green pepper rings, if desired. Makes 6 to 8 servings.

Fresh Tomato Vegetable Stew

This is a tasty and fast-fix vegetable stew that's made more rib–sticking with cheddar-tomato dumplings on top.

1 cup chopped onions	1/8 teaspoon pepper
1/4 cup butter or margarine, melted	2 cups peeled and cubed potatoes
4 cups fresh tomato wedges	1 1/2 cups cut fresh green beans
Boiling water	1 cup sliced fresh carrots
1 1/2 teaspoons salt	Cheddar-tomato dumplings (see
1/4 teaspoon sugar	recipe below)

In a large saucepan over medium high heat, cook onions in butter until limp and tender. Dip tomatoes in boiling water. Peel off skins. Cut tomatoes into wedges. Add tomatoes, salt, sugar, and pepper to onions. Lower heat. Cover and simmer for 20 minutes. Add potatoes, green beans, and carrots. Cover and cook for about 20 minutes or until vegetables are crisp-tender. Drop a tablespoon of dumpling dough over simmering stew. Cover and cook over medium-low heat for 10 to 15 minutes or until dumplings are firm. Makes 6 to 8 servings.

Cheddar-Tomato Dumplings

1 cup all-purpose flour	1/2 cup shredded cheddar cheese
3 tablespoons shortening	1/3 cup chopped tomatoes
1 1/2 teaspoons baking powder	1 tablespoon snipped parsley
1/4 teaspoon salt	6 tablespoons buttermilk

In a medium mixing bowl, combine flour, shortening, baking powder, and salt. Mix well, using pastry blender or two table knives until it resembles coarse crumbs. Stir in cheese, tomatoes, and parsley. Add buttermilk. Stir just until dry ingredients are moistened. Drop dumpling dough by tablespoon into your favorite stew recipe. Cook, covered, for 10 to 15 minutes or until dumplings are firm. Makes 6 to 8 servings.

Cherry Tomatoes in Dill

This is an attractive side dish as well as a tasty way to serve all those cherry tomatoes.

6 cups of cherry tomatoes
2 tablespoons butter or margarine
1 teaspoon salt
Dash of pepper
1 tablespoon fresh snipped dill
Several sprigs of fresh dill for garnish, optional

Remove green hulls from cherry tomatoes. Wash and wipe dry. In a large skillet, melt butter over very low heat. Add tomatoes; heat until barely warmed. Add salt, pepper, and dill. Shake skillet to thoroughly coat tomatoes. Continue to cook over very low heat for an additional 2 to 3 minutes or until tomatoes are warmed. Serve in a bowl topped with several sprigs of fresh dill, if desired. Makes about 4 to 6 servings.

Spiced Tomato Jam

Use up any end-of-season tomatoes in this spicy jam. It's terrific served on toast or crackers with either cream cheese or cheddar cheese.

6 1/2 pounds ripe fresh tomatoes, peeled, seeded, and cut into large chunks
1 1/2 large lemons, very thinly sliced, seeds removed
1 lime, very thinly sliced, seeds removed
3 1/2 cups sugar

1/2 cup apple cider vinegar
1 teaspoon coarse (kosher) salt
3/4 teaspoon ground allspice
3/4 teaspoon ground cloves
3/4 teaspoon ground ginger
1 teaspoon ground cinnamon
2 sticks cinnamon, each about 4-inches long

In a large (8-quart) kettle, combine tomatoes, lemons, lime, sugar, vinegar, and salt. Let stand for 1 hour at room temperature. Stir occasionally. Blend in allspice, cloves, ginger, and cinnamon. Let stand for an additional 15 minutes. Bring to a boil over medium-high heat. Stir occasionally. Add cinnamon sticks and blend into tomato mixture. Reduce heat and simmer, uncovered, 1 hour or more, until mixture is reduced to about 6 cups. As mixture thickens, stir constantly to avoid scorching. Ladle into sterilized jars, leaving 1/4-inch headroom. Run a rubber spatula around the insides of the jars to release trapped air bubbles. Wipe rims with a clean cloth. Place lids in position and tighten screw bands. Process in a bath of boiling water for 10 minutes. (The water should cover the jars by about 1 inch.) Cool on wire rack and store in a cool, dark place. Makes about 6 to 7 pint jars.

Green Tomato Relish

This delicious relish is made from end-of-the-season vegetables, just before first frost, when vines are laden with green tomatoes. The precise amount of each vegetable is not crucial, so don't worry if you have a little more or less of a particular vegetable, as long as you have a mix.

4 quarts washed, cored, and
   chopped green tomatoes
2 quarts chopped cabbage
2 cups chopped sweet red peppers
2 cups chopped onions
1 cup chopped sweet green
   peppers

$1/2$ cup salt
$4 1/2$ cups white vinegar
2 cups packed brown sugar
2 tablespoons mustard seed
1 tablespoon celery seed
1 tablespoon prepared horseradish

In a large container, combine tomatoes, cabbage, red peppers, onions, and green pepper. Sprinkle with salt and blend thoroughly. Let stand for 4 hours, stirring occasionally. Drain. Rinse and drain thoroughly, pressing to remove as much liquid as possible. In an 8-quart heavy kettle, combine vinegar, sugar, mustard seed, celery seed, and horseradish. Stir to blend. Bring mixture to a boil over medium-high heat and continue boiling for 15 minutes. Add tomato mixture and return to boiling. Lower heat and simmer for about 30 minutes or until cooked down and crisp-tender, with just enough liquid to moisten vegetables. Pack hot relish into hot jars leaving $1/4$-inch headroom. Adjust two-piece caps. Process 10 minutes in a boiling-water canner. Makes about 8 to 10 pints.

A U T U M N

Neighbors

Now I've met many others,
And many fine and true
But I can't seem to find one
That can compare with you.

With your smile of understanding
And your hand stretched out to aid
Oh, neighbor, 'tis in God's own garden
Nice folks like you are made.

Anne M. Diley (1916–1969)

Apple Butter Days

Recipes in This Chapter

What do you do with apples after you've made applesauce, apple pie, baked apples, apple cake, apple cookies, apple dumplings, and apple cobbler and canned more than a hundred quarts of the fruit?

You make apple butter. At least that's what my mother did after she looked out the kitchen window one morning and saw bruised and battered apples scattered on the grass, felled by a brisk wind.

"Windfalls?" Dad asked when she walked in, cradling apples in her apron.

"No. Apple butter," she answered, "Or they will be by evening. There's lots more apples under the trees, so we'd best get busy."

By the time I left for school the chore of coring and quartering to turn the windfalls into apple butter was underway.

Later that afternoon, the rich aroma of cooking apple butter greeted me long before I reached the kitchen door. I found Mother at the stove stirring a simmering kettle of dark burgundy apple butter. Unlike some of our neighbors, she didn't have a copper kettle or an outdoor fire pit for cooking her apple butter. Not that she didn't want one. It was just that she worked in smaller batches, using her flat-bottomed canning kettle over a low fire on her kitchen range and it worked fine.

Drawing in a deep breath to savor the heady aroma, I visualized it slathered on hot biscuits for supper. I couldn't resist asking, "How long does it have to cook?"

Mother shrugged. "It all depends on who you ask. Everyone has their own way of judging that, just like they have a way determining how much sugar it needs, what spices to use, and when to add them. The shorter the cooking time the softer the finished product. Cook it longer and it becomes firmer."

In spite of her constant stirring, the apple butter sputtered and popped. When I jumped back in surprise, she continued.

"Some cooks say to cook apple butter until cat eyes appear, plus fifteen minutes." She laughed at my puzzled expression and explained. "'Cat eyes' is such a hard boil that the bubbles keep bursting open like a cat's eye blinking at you." She pointed at the steaming kettle and said, "Just like it's doing now."

She dropped a large spoonful of apple butter on a saucer and gave it a critical look. "Looks like it's done," she said when no liquid ran from the edges. "But the best way to tell if it's finished cooking is to sample it." Handing me a spoonful, she waited for my reaction.

The flavor of the warm, spicy-sweet apple butter didn't disappoint me; it tasted as good as the aroma promised. When I nodded my approval, she pronounced it ready for the jars.

It took Mother several days to turn all the windfalls into apple butter. By the time she finished, more than fifty shiny pints rested on the basement shelves. During the winter months, we'd open them one by one and savor the apple butter on toast, pancakes, and best of all, on homemade bread. The perfect treat to find in our school lunchboxes!

Grandma's Old-Fashioned Apple Butter

The following is Mother's apple butter recipe just as she gave it to me. While she preferred using only stick cinnamon, small amounts of nutmeg, cloves, or allspice can be added to taste, if desired.

Wash, core, and quarter enough apples to fill a 16-quart kettle. Add 2 cups of water. Cook slowly over very low heat and stir constantly. Use a heavy kettle with a broad, flat bottom to allow the apples to bubble freely. When they are thoroughly cooked, cool slightly. Run through a food mill. There should be about 8 quarts of pulp. Measure 2 cups of sugar to 4 cups of apple pulp. Place mixture back in heavy kettle. Here the broad, flat kettle bottom allows the sugar and pulp to mix and cook freely. Add 10 2-inch cinnamon sticks. Use a wooden spoon or a flat paddle to stir the mixture constantly while it is cooking over very low heat. (The stirring allows the steam to escape and prevents scorching.) To check if it's done, place some apple butter on a cool saucer. If no rim of liquid forms around the edge of the butter, it's ready for the jar. Place in hot sterilized jars, leaving 1/2-inch head space. Seal at once by adjusting lids. Process pints 10 minutes in a boiling water bath. Makes about 12 pints.

Apple Dumplings with Cinnamon Sauce

This is a family-sized dessert, but it still disappears in a hurry.

Cinnamon Sauce

2 cups sugar
2 tablespoons all-purpose flour
2 tablespoons butter
1 tablespoon ground cinnamon
2 cups boiling water

In a medium bowl, combine sugar, flour, butter, and cinnamon. Stir to mix. Add boiling water. Stir until well blended. Makes about 4 cups.

Dough

Nonstick spray coating
2 cups all-purpose flour
2 1/4 teaspoons baking powder
1/4 teaspoon baking soda
1 teaspoon salt

1/3 cup plus 2 teaspoons shortening
3/4 cup buttermilk
4 cups finely diced apples
Vanilla ice cream, optional

Preheat oven to 350°. Spray a 3-quart casserole with nonstick spray coating. In a large mixing bowl, combine flour, baking powder, baking soda, and salt. Stir to blend. Cut in shortening with pastry blender until mixture resembles coarse meal. Stir in buttermilk. When thoroughly mixed, turn onto lightly floured surface and pat out to a 1/2-inch-thick rectangle. Spread with apples. Carefully roll up as for a jellyroll (apples will spill out, but you will tuck them in). Cut 2-inch slices off the roll. Place in prepared casserole. Tuck any and all extra spilled apples over slices or down around the sides. Pour hot cinnamon sauce over the apple roll slices. Bake for about 45 to 50 minutes or until apples are tender and dough is lightly browned. Serve with vanilla ice cream, if desired. Makes about 8 to 10 servings.

Apple Crisp

This is a hearty, homespun recipe that yields a tasty pudding-type dessert with a varied texture due to the crispy bits.

Nonstick spray coating
6–8 tart juicy apples
1/2 cup granulated sugar
1 cup uncooked rolled oats
1/2 cup all-purpose flour
3/4 cup packed brown sugar

2 teaspoons ground cinnamon, or to taste
1/2 cup butter
1/8 teaspoon ground nutmeg
Vanilla ice cream, optional

Preheat oven to 350°. Spray a 9 x 9 x 2-inch baking pan with nonstick spray coating. Peel, core, and slice apples and place them in prepared baking pan. Sprinkle with granulated sugar. In a small bowl, combine rolled oats, flour, brown sugar, and cinnamon. Cut in butter until mixture is crumbly. Spread rolled oats mixture over apples, pressing over top so it doesn't run off. Dust lightly with nutmeg. Bake for 35 to 40 minutes or until apples are tender and top is lightly browned. Serve warm with vanilla ice cream, if desired. Makes about 8 to 10 servings.

Fried Apples

This is a favorite side dish to serve with roast pork. You might only need the sugar if the apples are very tart.

3 tablespoons butter or margarine
6 cups tart apples, peeled, cored, and cut into 1/2-inch rounds
1/2 cup sugar, or as needed
1/2 teaspoon cinnamon

In a large skillet, melt butter over low heat. Layer apple slices in butter no more than 2 deep. Sprinkle with sugar and cinnamon to taste. Cook over low heat, stirring occasionally with a spatula, until apples are browned and tender. Remove fried slices and place on a warm platter. Repeat process with remaining apple slices. Serve warm. Makes about 5 to 6 servings.

Chunky Applesauce

This is a classic recipe—so simple, so good.

8 Cortland or McIntosh apples,
    peeled, cored, and cut into
    eighths
3/4 cup water, or more as needed

1/2 cup sugar, or to taste
1/8 teaspoon ground cinnamon
1/2 cup heavy cream for topping,
    optional

In a medium saucepan, combine apples and water. Cook covered, over medium heat, stirring occasionally until apples are tender and desired state of chunkiness has arrived. Pour into serving dish. Sugar to taste while still warm. Stir in cinnamon. Serve warm with cream, if desired. Makes about 4 to 6 servings.

NOTE:
For a completely different flavor, add 1 to 2 tablespoons horseradish, chopped mint, or finely chopped chives or fresh dill to 2 1/2 cups of unsweetened applesauce.

Fruit juices (orange, pineapple, apple) may be substituted for the 3/4 cup boiling water in the basic sauce.

A new texture and flavor can be accomplished with the addition of fresh fruit such as 1 cup fresh raspberries or 2 cups sliced fresh strawberries.

Deep Dish Ham 'n' Apples

This oven-baked dish is simple to prepare for family or guests.

Nonstick spray coating
3 cups ground cooked ham
1/2 teaspoon dry mustard
3 tablespoons minced onion
1 beaten egg
1/2 cup milk

1 cup soft bread crumbs
4 large tart apples, peeled and
   cored
1/4 cup packed brown sugar
2 tablespoons melted butter or
   margarine

Preheat oven to 350°. Spray a 2-quart casserole with nonstick spray coating. In a large mixing bowl, combine ham, mustard, onion, egg, milk, and bread crumbs. Stir until well mixed. Turn into prepared casserole. Slice apples about 1/2 inch thick. Arrange apples over ham mixture, overlapping slices around edges of dish. Sprinkle apples with brown sugar and butter. Bake uncovered for about 40 minutes or until apple slices are browned and tender. Makes about 6 to 8 servings.

Main Dish Apple Salad

Cortlands have a very white inside with a red skin that looks attractive when chopped in a salad. Their tartness complements celery and mayonnaise.

2 teaspoons lemon juice
2 cups unpeeled, diced Cortland
   apples
1 cup diced cheddar cheese
1 cup uncooked elbow macaroni,
   cooked and drained
1 cup leftover diced chicken
1 cup diced celery

$1/3$ cup minced green pepper
$1/3$ cup minced sweet red pepper
$1/3$ cup minced green onion
$1/2$ cup mayonnaise
2 tablespoons milk
$1/2$ teaspoon salt
$1/4$ teaspoon dry mustard

In a large mixing bowl, drizzle lemon juice over apples. Combine apples with cheese, macaroni, chicken, celery, green and red peppers, and onion. Stir to mix. In a small bowl, combine mayonnaise with milk, salt, and mustard. Stir until blended and smooth. Combine mayonnaise mixture with apple mixture. Stir until all ingredients are moistened. Cover and chill for 2 to 3 hours to allow flavors to blend. Makes about 8 to 10 servings.

Apple Kuchen

This is a wonderful addition to the breakfast table or any other meal.

Nonstick spray coating
2 cups all-purpose flour
2 teaspoons baking powder
1 teaspoon salt
$3/4$ cup sugar
$1/3$ cup shortening
1 beaten egg

1 cup milk
1 teaspoon vanilla
6 large tart apples, peeled, cored,
    and cut into $1/4$-inch slices
2 tablespoons sugar for topping
$1/2$ teaspoon cinnamon

Preheat oven to 350°. Spray an 11 x 7 x 1 $1/2$-inch baking pan with nonstick spray coating. In a medium bowl, combine flour, baking powder, and salt. Stir to mix. In a large mixing bowl, cream together sugar and shortening. Add egg and beat until light and fluffy. Combine milk and vanilla. Add to creamed mixture alternately with flour. Stir until just blended. Pour batter into prepared baking pan. Arrange and overlap apple slices in rows over batter. Combine sugar and cinnamon and sprinkle over apples. Bake for 35 to 40 minutes or until apples are tender and a toothpick inserted in center comes out clean. Serve warm or cold. Makes about 8 to 10 servings.

Raisin Apple-Butter Pie

In this rich pie, plump raisins are surrounded by spicy apple butter.

Unbaked single crust pastry shell
   (see recipe, page 37)
1 1/2 cups raisins
Boiling water
2 well-beaten eggs
1 cup apple butter
1/3 cup sugar

1/4 teaspoon salt
1 teaspoon vanilla
1/4 teaspoon baking soda
1 cup buttermilk
Sweetened whipped cream for
   topping, optional

Preheat oven to 375°. Cover raisins with boiling water. Let stand for about 10 minutes until raisins are plump. Drain well. In a large mixing bowl, combine eggs, apple butter, sugar, salt, and vanilla. Mix well. Stir baking soda into buttermilk. Fold buttermilk and raisins into apple butter mixture. Pour into prepared pie shell. Bake for 10 minutes. Lower heat to 350°. Continue baking for 40 minutes longer or until knife inserted in center comes out clean. Cool before cutting. Serve with a dollop of whipped cream, if desired. Makes about 8 servings.

Feeding the Silo Fillers

Recipes in This Chapter

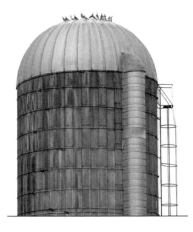

It always seemed that when school started in the fall, the curtain of summer fell. A whole new set of sights, aromas, and sounds embraced us. Almost overnight, the maples donned their golden skirts of yellow, tangerine, and rust. The sumac flashed their spikes of red and the goldfinches put on their drab winter coats.

As the sun-warmed days of autumn gave way to blanket-required nights, Dad's crops ripened in the fields and Mother's garden reached maturity. We no longer ate fresh-picked peas, beans, or cucumbers. The tomato plants needed nightly covering against the first nip of frost. Canning in the kitchen slowed and finally came to an end.

Then, before Mother could draw a breath and relax, Dad announced, "Corn's ready. We'll be filling silo in a day or two."

Silo filling meant exchanging help with the neighbors. Mother's friends, Viv and Marie, arrived to lend a needed hand with the cooking. Mother enjoyed preparing meals for the silo fillers as much as she did for threshers. She welcomed the changing seasons and the opportunity to serve what she called "fall vegetables."

Along with the hearty meat-and-potato dishes, she prepared cabbage salads, squash, and rutabagas to serve on the side. Her desserts also changed with the seasons, from berries and shortcakes to spicy gingerbreads.

"Gingerbread always tastes better in the fall," she maintained, "especially on a crisp day."

Mother's kitchen windows faced the farmyard, with both silos in plain view. However, she didn't really need to look outside to know what was going on. She relied on keen hearing and a sixth sense most farm wives acquire. Without a glance toward the window, she knew when the wagons pulled up to the silo, whose team pulled the wagon, when the cornstalks went in, when the pipes plugged up—and the minute things began running right again.

And she knew without being told when there was trouble in the field, a breakdown, or worse, an accident. Like the time the binder jammed and my father reached in to pull out the stalks. The arm of the freshly cleared binder caught his shirt sleeve and jerked him in. Luckily, men on a nearby wagon saw what happened and rushed to his aid. He escaped with an injured forearm. After spending several days in the hospital, he returned home to heal.

The cycle of harvesting continued without slowing in the warm, hazy days of Indian summer. The neighbors all pitched in to finish filling Dad's silos. That's the way of country folks: Neighbors helping neighbors.

Poppy Seed Slaw

Poppy seeds add a nice touch to the already colorful mix of red and green cabbage. Add the sweet-sour taste of honey-vinegar dressing, and you have an appealing salad.

3 cups shredded red cabbage	2 tablespoons salad oil
3 cups shredded green cabbage	2 tablespoons poppy seeds
3 carrots, shredded	1 teaspoon salt
1/2 cup honey	1 teaspoon dry mustard
1/2 cup cider vinegar	1/4 teaspoon onion powder

In a large bowl, combine red and green cabbage and carrots. In a screw-top jar, combine honey, vinegar, salad oil, poppy seeds, salt, mustard, and onion powder. Cover and shake well. Pour dressing over cabbage mixture; toss to coat. Cover and chill 1 to 24 hours. Makes about 6 to 8 servings.

Beef and Garlic Pork Loin Roast

This was one of Mother's favorite ways to serve roasts, especially when she had a crew to feed. The blended flavors of beef and pork produce a rich, brown gravy. Leftovers, served cold, make excellent sandwiches.

    1 3- to 4-pound boneless chuck roast
    1 3- to 4-pound boneless pork loin roast
    2 tablespoons cooking oil
    Salt and pepper, to taste
    4 cloves peeled garlic

Preheat oven to 325°. In a large skillet over medium high heat, brown meat on all sides in hot oil. Drain fat. Place meat, fatty side up, in 15 1/2 x 10 1/2 x 2-inch roast pan. Rub surface of both roasts with salt and pepper. Make 4 deep slits in the pork roast. Slide a clove of garlic into each opening. Insert meat thermometers in meatiest part of the roasts. Roast, uncovered, for 2 1/2 to 3 hours or until meat thermometer registers 170° for pork and 140° to 170° for beef, depending on degree of doneness desired. Baste occasionally with pan juices during last hour of roasting. Lift roast to warm platter and cover with foil to keep warm. Let rest for 5 to 10 minutes before slicing. Serve warm with pan gravy. Makes about 10 to 12 servings.

To Make Gravy

Leaving crusty bits in roasting pan, pour off meat juices and fat into a large measuring cup. Skim off fat, leaving 3 to 4 tablespoons of juice. Add water to make 2 cups of liquid. Return mixture to pan. In a small bowl, mix 3 tablespoons all-purpose flour and 1/4 cup water. Mix until smooth and lump free. Add to cooking liquid and cook, stirring constantly, for 2 to 3 minutes or until thickened and bubbly. Season with salt and pepper to taste. Makes about 2 cups.

Paprika Chicken

Mother's flock of chickens kept the family supplied with eggs and meat. While she prepared many delicious chicken dishes, this was our favorite for dinner or supper. It also made a hit with both the silo fillers and dinner guests.

1 3- to 4-pound fryer
3 tablespoons shortening
2 cups finely chopped onions
1 green pepper, cut into $1/2$-inch slices
2–3 tablespoons sweet Hungarian paprika, or to taste

1 teaspoon salt
1 cup sour cream
Cooked noodles
Parsley for garnish, optional

Disjoint and cut chicken into serving-size pieces. Wash and pat dry. In a large skillet, heat shortening over medium-high heat. Sauté onions and green pepper until tender but not browned. Reduce heat to low. Add chicken pieces. Sprinkle paprika over chicken until all pieces are well coated. Sprinkle with salt. Cover and cook slowly for 1 hour or until chicken is tender, occasionally turning pieces over so they will cook evenly. If necessary, add small amounts of water. When chicken is done, add sour cream. Cover and heat slowly for 2 to 3 minutes to just warm the sour cream. Serve with freshly boiled noodles. Garnish with parsley, if desired. Makes 5 to 6 servings.

Rutabaga with Onions in Sour Cream

Rutabagas were always a favorite vegetable in Mother's country kitchen. She especially liked to serve this dish with her pork roasts.

1 chicken bouillon cube	2 tablespoons butter
1/2 cup boiling water	1/2 teaspoon salt
1 large rutabaga, peeled and cut	1/8 teaspoon pepper
into 1/2-inch cubes (about 4 cups)	1 cup sour cream
3 cups chopped onions	Dash of paprika for garnish, optional
1/2 cup diced celery	

In a small bowl, dissolve bouillon cube in boiling water. In a large saucepan, combine bouillon broth and rutabaga. Cover and cook until rutabaga is crisp-tender for about 15 minutes. Meanwhile, in a medium skillet, sauté onions and celery in butter until crisp-tender. Stir in salt and pepper. Add onion mixture to rutabaga. Gently stir to blend vegetables. Fold in sour cream to coat vegetables. Serve warm with a sprinkle of paprika, if desired. Makes about 6 to 8 servings.

Pork and Butternut Squash

Here's a perfect autumn dish that's easy enough for family meals and special enough for company.

2 pounds pork tenderloin, cut into
   1 1/2-inch cubes
3 tablespoons vegetable oil, or more
   as needed
3 cups sliced onions
2–2 1/2 pounds butternut squash,
   peeled and cut into 1-inch cubes

1 12-ounce can of beer
1 teaspoon salt
1/4 teaspoon pepper
1/4 teaspoon ground rosemary,
   optional

In a large Dutch oven, over medium-high heat, brown pork cubes in oil. Lower heat to medium. Add onions and sauté until onions are limp. Add the squash and stir to blend. Slowly add only enough beer to provide cooking moisture. (As the mixture cooks, you may need to add the entire can.) Sprinkle with salt, pepper, and rosemary, if desired. Cover and allow the pork mixture to simmer until meat and squash are tender. Stir occasionally to blend the mixture while being careful to allow the squash to retain as much of its shape as possible. Serve warm. Makes about 8 to 10 servings.

German Rye Bread

Hearty and wholesome, this recipe combines white and rye flour and is flavored with molasses and caraway seeds.

3 cups all-purpose flour
1/4 cup unsweetened cocoa powder
2 packages active dry yeast
3 tablespoons crushed caraway
    seeds
2 cups water
1/3 cup dark molasses
2 tablespoons butter or margarine,
    softened

1 tablespoon sugar
1 tablespoon salt
3–3 1/2 cups rye flour
Nonstick spray coating
Cornmeal, as needed
Melted butter, as needed

In a large mixer bowl, combine all-purpose flour, cocoa powder, dry yeast, and caraway seeds. Stir to blend. In a medium saucepan, combine water, molasses, butter, sugar, and salt. Heat until just warm (115° to 120°). Add to dry mixture. Beat at low speed of electric mixer 1/2 minute, scraping sides of bowl constantly. Beat at high speed for 3 minutes. With a spoon, stir in enough rye flour to make a soft dough. Turn out onto a lightly floured surface. Knead for 5 to 6 minutes or until smooth and elastic. Shape into a ball. Place in greased bowl and turn once to grease the top surface. Cover. Let rest in a warm place free from draft for 20 minutes. Spray a large baking sheet with nonstick spray coating and sprinkle with cornmeal. Punch down and divide dough in half. Knead several times. Shape each half into a round loaf. Place on baking sheet at least 4 inches apart. Brush surface with melted butter. Slash tops of loaves with a sharp knife. Cover. Let rise again in a warm place, free from draft for 50 to 60 minutes or until doubled. Preheat oven to 400°. Bake in preheated oven for 25 to 30 minutes or until browned and loaves sound hollow when tapped. Remove from baking sheet and cool on wire racks. Makes 2 round loaves.

Raisin Gingerbread

The raisins nestle into the spicy batter, adding a light touch of flavor.

Nonstick spray coating
1 cup sugar
1 cup shortening, softened
1 cup dark molasses
2 teaspoons ground ginger
1 teaspoon ground cinnamon
1/4 teaspoon ground cloves
1/2 teaspoon salt
3 beaten eggs

3 cups all-purpose flour
1 cup boiling water, divided
2 teaspoons baking soda
1 cup raisins
Lemon whipped cream for topping,
    optional (see recipe, page 141)
Lemon crème sauce for topping,
    optional (see recipe, page 141)

Preheat oven to 350°. Spray a 13 x 9 x 2-inch baking pan with nonstick spray coating. In a large mixing bowl, combine sugar and shortening. Beat until light and fluffy. Stir in molasses, ginger, cinnamon, cloves, and salt. Mix thoroughly. Add eggs and flour. Beat for several minutes or until thoroughly mixed. Blend in boiling water, reserving 1 tablespoon. Dissolve baking soda in reserved water. Stir into molasses mixture until well blended. Pour about 2/3 of the mixture into prepared baking pan. Scatter raisins evenly over the batter. Cover with the remaining batter. Bake 40 to 45 minutes or until toothpick inserted in center comes out clean. Serve plain or with sweetened lemon whipped cream or lemon crème sauce, if desired. Makes about 8 to 10 servings.

Lemon Whipped Cream

1 cup heavy cream
2 teaspoons powdered sugar
1 teaspoon lemon extract

In a medium bowl, beat cream with electric mixer or rotary beater until frothy. Gradually beat in sugar and lemon extract. Continue beating until stiff peaks form. Makes about 1 cup.

Lemon Crème Sauce

1 cup sugar
2 1/2 tablespoons cornstarch
1/4 teaspoon salt
2 cups water

2 slightly beaten egg yolks
1 tablespoon lemon peel
1/2 cup lemon juice
1/4 cup soft butter

In a medium saucepan, combine sugar, cornstarch, and salt. Gradually add water and blend in until smooth. Cook over medium heat, stirring constantly until mixture is thick and clear. Remove from heat. Blend about 1/2 cup of hot mixture into egg yolks. Stir to blend. Add to hot mixture in saucepan. Cook for 2 minutes, stirring constantly. Add lemon peel, lemon juice, and butter. Stir to blend until butter melts. Serve warm or cold. Makes about 2 3/4 cups.

Cabbage to Kraut

Recipes in This Chapter

By the time September greets October, the vivid glow is off the maples and only bronze leaves rustle under foot. We embrace the warm days of Indian summer and ignore the chilly nights. By the time fuzzy caterpillars inch along and geese begin their journey south, the corn harvest is in full swing.

The morning I came down to breakfast and found Mother scrubbing a 12-gallon crock within an inch of its life, dousing it with boiling water and repeating the process, I knew for sure autumn was upon us and sauerkraut season about to begin.

Making sauerkraut was a long-standing tradition in our country kitchen. Since we all enjoyed eating it in a number of different ways, putting up with the fermenting inconvenience seemed a minor point—to Mother.

For as long as I can remember, she insisted that making sauerkraut was a family affair. "Many hands make light work," she claimed.

Of course Dad held the same belief when it came to harvesting his potato crop. But at least once they were dug, bagged, and carried to the basement bins, his potatoes didn't reek with a penetrating aroma as fermenting cabbage did.

Right after breakfast, Dad brought his huge wheelbarrow full of fresh-cut cabbage heads up to the back door. Grandma met him there with a sharp knife. In a flash, she trimmed off the outer leaves, checked for spoiled spots, and split the heads into halves and quarters, depending on the size. I hauled the split heads to the kitchen table, where Mother was adjusting the long rectangular kraut cutter with its two slanted steel blades over the waiting crock.

Everything in position, Mother snatched up a section of cabbage and began the rhythmic back and forth motion required to shred the heads thinner than a dime. A shower of slivered cabbage drifted down into the crock. The tedious process continued all morning, with the adults relieving one another on the kraut cutter.

"Watch your fingers, that cutter's sharp," became the morning's litany each time they changed positions. As the shredded cabbage built up in the crock, Mother sprinkled coarse canning salt over each layer. Handing me a heavy wooden mallet, she ordered, "Pound it down good. Or, as Grandma says, smush it until the juices cover the cabbage. That's what makes the brine so it can ferment."

When she finally called a halt to my pounding, she announced, "Tasting time." The three adults reached into the crock to taste the raw cabbage to check the salt content. Satisfied, we resumed our cut-shred-salt-pound-taste routine. It was a tossup as to which part was more exhausting.

By midafternoon, shredded and pounded cabbage filled the crock to within four inches of the top, and Mother declared it full enough. Sweating and speckled with salty kraut juice and cabbage bits, we stood back and admired our work. Mother slipped a cheesecloth over the cabbage and lapped it over the edge of the crock. Dad fit a snug wooden disk and weight over the covering. The crock with its contents was left in the corner of the kitchen to do its own thing. And boy did it.

In the first week, we more or less ignored the crock. Mother checked it daily, replacing the cheesecloth with a fresh one, skimming off the rising brine and any mold that formed. What started as an acceptable aroma floating in the air, quickly turned distinctively unpleasant. By the start of the second week, there was no way we could forget the crock of fermenting cabbage "working" in the corner.

For the next five to six weeks, first the kitchen, then the entire house, took on a whole new aroma. Weird smells that no room deodorant or frying fish could mask swirled in the air. On sunny days we opened windows and doors to clear the air, but that didn't work on chilly evenings.

When we complained about the aroma, Mother brushed our protests and suggestions aside. "It needs to be in the warm kitchen to work," she said. "The basement and garage are too cold for it to properly ferment. Have patience, it's coming along nicely."

Dad, meanwhile, grumbled and threatened to toss the entire works out to the hogs. "The only thing stopping me," he said, "was the fear of having a drunken hog on my hands. Next year, we buy all our sauerkraut."

Never once during this time did I have any friends over to our house; I was afraid if they caught even a faint whiff of the fermenting cabbage, they'd think terrible things about Mother's housekeeping. All after-meal conversation ceased; the men simply ate and ran. Dad stopped inviting salesmen into the house; he did all his visiting and business on the back porch or in the barn. Even Mother didn't welcome any of her friends in for coffee; after one visit, drop-in company stopped dropping in.

Meanwhile, the fermenting cabbage kept merrily working. About the sixth week, we heard strange noises coming from the crock. Something definitely wanted to get out. It bubbled and blistered, gurgled and fizzed, sending roiling brine over the top and down the sides of the crock, taking the finish off Mother's new linoleum. She merely smiled and reassured us, "It's coming along nicely."

Then, after what seemed like twelve months in seven weeks, there came a day Mother couldn't find any more bubbles. She declared the sauerkraut done and ready to eat and package for the freezer. The crock disappeared from the corner of the kitchen. However, the pungent smell lingered a while longer.

Before long we reclaimed our normal country kitchen routine, filling the air with the savory aromas of baking bread and beef roasts. Once Mother began serving fresh sauerkraut we'd more or less forgotten the offensive smell and enjoyed the delicious kraut dishes she placed before us.

One day at dinner over a dish of pork hocks and sauerkraut, we heard Dad boasting to a visiting salesman, "There is nothing like homemade kraut. Next year we plan to make a double batch."

My brothers and I looked at each other and rolled our eyes.

Hungarian Sauerkraut Soup

Anyone who likes sauerkraut with their brats will enjoy this delicious soup. It makes a satisfying meal—warm, tasty, and filling—day or night.

2 cups of finely chopped sauerkraut
1/4 pound bacon, cut into small pieces
1 medium onion, finely chopped
2 tablespoons sweet Hungarian paprika
2 quarts water

1 pound smoked sausage, cut into 1/4-inch slices
1/2 cup sour cream, room temperature
1/4 cup all-purpose flour
Salt, optional

Rinse sauerkraut in a colander under cold water. Drain well. Transfer sauerkraut to a large Dutch oven. Set aside. In a small skillet, slowly fry bacon until almost crisp. Add the bacon pieces to the sauerkraut. Sauté the onion in bacon fat until it turns translucent. Add the onion to the sauerkraut. Add paprika, water, and sausage to the sauerkraut mixture. Mix well. Bring to a boil. Reduce heat and simmer, covered, for 35 minutes. In a small bowl, stir the sour cream into the flour. Blend about 3 tablespoons of soup into the sour cream mixture, then slowly pour it into the hot soup. Simmer for 5 minutes or until the flour has a chance to cook and thicken the soup slightly. Do not allow the soup to boil, as the sour cream will curdle. Taste and add salt, if desired. The soup should be very sharp and sour. Makes about 6 to 8 servings.

Sauerkraut Potato Salad

The tangy flavor of sauerkraut gives a delightful lift to traditional potato salad. This is perfect for a summer picnic.

2 cups well-drained sauerkraut
4 cups cooked, sliced potatoes
2 hard-boiled eggs, chopped
1/4 cup diced green pepper
1/4 cup diced sweet red pepper
3/4 cup mayonnaise
1/4 cup sour cream

2 tablespoons sugar
1 teaspoon dry mustard
1 teaspoon sweet paprika
1/2 teaspoon salt
1/8 teaspoon pepper
Parsley for garnish, optional

In a large mixing bowl, combine sauerkraut, potatoes, eggs, and green and red peppers. Toss gently to mix. Chill. In a small bowl, combine mayonnaise, sour cream, sugar, mustard, paprika, salt, and pepper. Mix well. Pour over salad and toss lightly to thoroughly coat potatoes. Adjust seasonings to taste. Chill and serve cold. Makes about 6 to 8 servings.

Country Spareribs and Sauerkraut

Sharp and savory sauerkraut pairs nicely with pork, especially when served with baked potatoes.

1 1/2 to 2 pounds country style
   spareribs
2 tablespoons shortening
1 cup chopped onions

1 tablespoon sugar, optional
3–3 1/2 cups sauerkraut, undrained
1 teaspoon caraway seeds
1/2 cup water

Preheat oven to 350°. In a large skillet, brown spareribs in shortening. Place browned spareribs in a large casserole or Dutch oven. Set aside. In the same skillet, sauté onion until tender. Stir in sugar, sauerkraut, and caraway seeds. Layer onion/sauerkraut mixture over spareribs. Add water to skillet drippings and pour over sauerkraut. Cover. Bake for 1 1/2 to 2 hours or until spareribs are tender. Serve hot. Makes about 4 to 6 servings.

Hot Dogs with Sauerkraut

Here is a simple, quick dish Mother prepared when time-challenged. It can be served as is or in a bun, making it a family favorite with kids of all ages.

2 tablespoons butter or margarine
1 small onion, diced
1/2 cup diced celery
3–3 1/2 cups well-drained sauerkraut
1/2 teaspoon caraway seeds
1 pound frankfurters
Buns, optional

In a Dutch oven over moderate heat, melt butter and sauté onion and celery until crisp-tender. Add sauerkraut and caraway seeds. Stir to mix evenly. Layer frankfurters over sauerkraut mixture. Cover and cook 15 to 18 minutes or until thoroughly heated. Makes about 4 to 5 servings.

NOTE: For variety, omit caraway seeds from the above recipe. Add 2 cups stewed tomatoes and 1 teaspoon paprika along with the sauerkraut. Just before serving, top frankfurters with 1/2 cup shredded cheddar cheese. Cover and simmer 5 minutes or until cheese is melted. Makes about 4 to 5 servings.

Chocolate Cherry Surprise Cake

The surprise in this old-time country kitchen recipe is . . . sauerkraut! In a cake? Yes. You won't be able to taste it, but the sauerkraut creates an extra-moist and slightly crunchy texture, making it a perfect complement for the rich chocolate flavor.

Nonstick spray coating
$2/3$ cup rinsed and well-drained sauerkraut
$2 1/4$ cups all-purpose flour
$1/2$ cup unsweetened cocoa powder
1 teaspoon baking powder
1 teaspoon baking soda
1 teaspoon salt
$1 1/2$ cups sugar

$2/3$ cup butter or margarine
3 eggs
$1/2$ teaspoon vanilla
1 cup cold water
$1/2$ cup drained and chopped maraschino cherries
$1/2$ cup chopped pecans
Chocolate cream cheese frosting (see recipe, page 149)

Preheat oven to 350°. Spray a 13 x 9 x 2-inch baking pan with nonstick spray coating. Squeeze all excess moisture from the sauerkraut with your hands. Using a kitchen shears, snip sauerkraut into fine pieces, or chop it with a knife. Set aside. In a medium bowl, combine flour, cocoa powder, baking powder, baking soda, and salt. Mix well. In a large mixing bowl, cream sugar and butter until light and fluffy. Add eggs, one at a time, beating well after each addition. Beat in vanilla. Gradually add flour mixture to cream mixture alternately with water. Stir in sauerkraut, cherries, and pecans. Turn batter into prepared baking pan. Bake for 30 to 35 minutes or until toothpick inserted in center comes out clean. Cool on wire rack. Frost with chocolate cream cheese frosting or your favorite frosting. Makes about 12 to 15 servings.

Chocolate Cream Cheese Frosting

1 1-ounce square semisweet chocolate
1 3-ounce package cream cheese, softened
1/2 teaspoon vanilla
1/8 teaspoon salt
1–1 1/2 cups powdered sugar
1 tablespoon milk

Melt chocolate over hot water. Cool slightly. In a medium bowl, combine chocolate, cream cheese, vanilla, and salt. Stir to blend. Add sugar alternately with milk and beat until smooth and of a spreading consistency, adding additional sugar as needed. Makes enough to frost the top of a 13 x 9 x 2-inch cake or the tops of two 8- or 9-inch cake layers.

Under the Hickory Nut Trees

Recipes in This Chapter

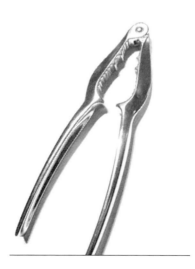

Nothing made my father smile faster than finding a grove of hickory trees in the woodlot of the new farm we'd just moved to. "We'll have a great time picking nuts in the fall," he said, beaming.

Dad enjoyed picking all sorts of wild things: blackberries, grapes, elderberries, mushrooms. The hickory trees simply extended his picking season. All summer he checked the developing nuts. Finally one Sunday afternoon in early October, he handed Mother and me a bucket and invited us to go pickin' nuts with him.

We wandered about the woodlot seeking out the best trees and gathering up the biggest nuts. Many times we'd merely sift through the grass and leaves under a hickory tree to fill our buckets. Other times we'd venture under a nearby thorn thicket to retrieve meaty nuts.

A hickory tree's fruit grows embraced in a thick, golf ball-sized green hull. It only takes a gentle autumn breeze to send a flutter of leaves dancing to the ground. Then ripe nuts fall like a splattering of hailstones, some opening at contact with the ground while others remain cuddled in their hulls.

Lulled by the warm sunshine and the occasional dull thudding of falling nuts, the peaceful woodlot didn't remain quiet for long. A crow sounded the first alarm, then a blue jay's raucous scolding jarred the air. We ignored them both.

However, the chattering and scolding squirrel perched on a maple branch several trees over caused us to look up and laugh at his antics.

"Don't worry, we'll leave some for you," Dad promised as we picked up our buckets and headed for home.

Pickin' hickory nuts on a sunny October afternoon is the fun part. The hard part comes later. It's the sorting, cracking, and meat picking that is time consuming.

Once back home, Dad spread the nuts on a canvas on the back porch to cure. After a week or so, we gathered them into a basket to wait for cracking.

No doubt about it, hickory nuts are hard to crack. One sharp smack with a hammer can scatter sharp shells in all directions. There are, of course, some helpful tricks. One of Dad's favorites was to pour boiling water over a kettle of whole nuts. He let them stand 10 to 15 minutes, or until the water cooled, before draining. He then dried off the surface moisture in a slow oven. Holding the nut between his thumb and forefinger, he held the rounded side up and cracked them in a vise. Most of the time he managed to split the hard shell rather than shatter it.

"Looking over the hickory nuts" took place with the entire family around the kitchen table after supper dishes were done. The goal was to pick out as many whole halves as possible. It takes time and effort to extract the tiny nuggets from the shell. In fact, it was a bit too tedious for most of us and Mother often ended up alone.

Hickory nuts have a unique taste. Some say it resembles a cross between a walnut and a pecan. Others insist it has a dark, smoky flavor. In any case, its distinctive taste is pleasing.

While Dad was the hickory nut picker and cracker in our family, Mother was the baker. She used hickory nuts in all her recipes calling for nuts. All became family favorites.

Hickory Nut Pumpkin Cake

To add a fun fall touch, garnish this cake with candy pumpkins.

Nonstick spray coating
2 1/4 cups all-purpose flour
3 teaspoons baking powder
1/2 teaspoon salt
1/4 teaspoon baking soda
1 1/2 teaspoons ground cinnamon
1/2 teaspoon ground ginger
1/2 teaspoon ground allspice
1/2 cup butter or margarine

1 cup packed brown sugar
1/2 cup granulated sugar
1 egg
2 egg yolks
3/4 cup buttermilk or sour milk
3/4 cup canned pumpkin
1/2 cup finely chopped hickory nuts
Cream cheese frosting, optional (see
    recipe below)

Preheat oven to 350°. Spray a 13 x 9 x 2-inch baking pan with nonstick spray coating. In a medium bowl, combine flour, baking powder, salt, baking soda, cinnamon, ginger, and allspice. Blend well. In a large mixer bowl, cream together butter, brown sugar, and granulated sugar. Beat until light and fluffy. Add egg and egg yolks, one at a time, beating after each until light and fluffy. Add flour mixture alternately with buttermilk, beating after each addition until smooth. Stir in pumpkin and nuts. Mix well. Pour into prepared baking pan. Bake for 30 to 35 minutes or until toothpick inserted in center comes out clean. Cool on wire rack. When cool, frost with cream cheese frosting, if desired. Makes about 12 to 15 servings.

Cream Cheese Frosting

8 ounces cream cheese, softened
1 cup butter, softened
2 cups powdered sugar
1 teaspoon vanilla
1/4 cup finely crushed hickory nuts

In a medium bowl, combine cream cheese and butter. Beat until well blended. Gradually add 1/4 cup powdered sugar at a time, beating well after each addition until mixture is smooth and fluffy. Stir in vanilla. Spread evenly on cake. Dust with hickory nuts. Makes about 3 cups, or enough to frost a 13 x 9 x 2-inch cake or enough to fill and frost an 8- or 9-inch layer cake.

Grandma D's Hickory Nut Coffee Cake

This old-fashioned recipe is a cross between a coffee cake and a sweet bread.

1/2 cup sugar
1/2 cup butter
2 teaspoons salt
2 cups scalded milk
1/2 cup lukewarm water
2 packages active dry yeast
3 beaten eggs

7–7 1/2 cups all-purpose flour
1/2 cup sugar for filling
2 teaspoons ground cinnamon
1/3 cup melted butter, divided
1 1/2 cups chopped hickory nuts,
   divided

In a large mixing bowl, combine sugar, 1/2 cup butter, and salt. Add milk and cool to lukewarm. In a small bowl, dissolve yeast in lukewarm water. When milk has cooled, stir yeast into milk mixture. Blend in eggs. Stir in 3 cups flour, mixing well. Stir in enough of remaining flour until the mixture becomes hard to stir. Turn out onto a lightly floured surface and knead, adding more flour as necessary, for 6 to 8 minutes or until dough is shiny and smooth. Clean the bowl, grease, and return dough to it. Turn once to coat top. Cover and let rise 1 to 1 1/2 hours or until doubled. Meanwhile, grease two baking pans. In a small bowl, combine sugar and cinnamon. Turn out dough onto a lightly floured surface. Divide dough in half. Pat first portion of dough out into a large oval. Spread with half of the melted butter. Sprinkle with sugar-cinnamon mixture. Top with half of the hickory nuts. Use a rolling pin to gently press nuts into dough. Carefully roll dough up jellyroll fashion. Shape into a large "U" shape. Place on prepared baking sheet, seam side down. Repeat with second half of dough, saving a small portion of melted butter to brush over tops of prepared dough. Cover and let rise 45 minutes or until doubled. Preheat oven to 350°. Bake in preheated oven for 35 to 40 minutes or until golden brown. Makes 2 large coffee cakes.

Hickory Nut Pumpkin Pie

Hickory nuts lend their unique flavor and a touch of elegance to this old-fashioned pumpkin pie.

Unbaked 10-inch pastry shell (see recipe, page 37)
2 tablespoons flour
1 1/2 teaspoons ground cinnamon
1/2 teaspoon salt
1/2 teaspoon ground ginger
1/2 teaspoon ground nutmeg
2 beaten eggs

1/2 cup packed brown sugar
1/2 cup granulated sugar
2 cups canned pumpkin
2 cups milk
3/4 cup coarsely chopped hickory nuts
Sweetened whipped cream for topping, optional

Preheat oven to 450°. In a small bowl, combine flour, cinnamon, salt, ginger, and nutmeg. In a large mixing bowl, combine eggs, brown sugar, and granulated sugar. Beat well. Stir in pumpkin and milk. Stir flour mixture into pumpkin mixture. Beat well. Pour into unbaked pie shell with a high, fluted rim. Sprinkle nuts over the top and lightly swirl them in. Bake for 10 minutes. Lower heat to 350° and continue baking for 40 minutes longer or until a knife inserted in center comes out clean. Cool on wire rack. Serve topped with a dollop of sweetened whipped cream, if desired. Makes 1 10-inch pie, about 8 to 10 servings.

Spiced Hickory Nuts

This is a special treat for snacking or to toss in salads.

2 cups hickory nut halves
$1/4$ cup butter
$1/8$ teaspoon cayenne pepper
$1/4$ teaspoon garlic salt
Seasoned salt, to taste

Preheat oven to 250°. On a large baking sheet, spread hickory nuts out in a thin layer. Dot with butter. Bake for 1 hour, stirring occasionally until nicely browned. Remove from oven. Season with cayenne pepper, garlic powder, and seasoned salt to taste. Stir and let cool. Store in a tin. Makes about 2 cups.

Hickory Nut Oatmeal Cookies

These cookies are nicely spiced and soft. Store airtight to retain freshness.

2 cups all-purpose flour
2 teaspoons baking powder
1 teaspoon salt
$1/4$ teaspoon baking soda
1 teaspoon ground cinnamon
1 teaspoon ground nutmeg
1 cup butter, softened
$1 1/2$ cups packed brown sugar
2 beaten eggs
$1/2$ cup milk
2 cups uncooked rolled oats
2 cups raisins
$3/4$ cup chopped hickory nuts

Preheat oven to 375°. In a medium bowl, combine flour, baking powder, salt, baking soda, cinnamon, and nutmeg. Stir to mix. In a large mixing bowl, combine butter and brown sugar. Beat until light and fluffy. Add eggs and beat until thoroughly combined. Add flour mixture to creamed mixture alternately with milk, beginning and ending with flour. Stir in oats, raisins, and hickory nuts. Blend well. Drop by rounded teaspoonfuls 2-inches apart onto ungreased cookie sheet. Bake for 8 to 10 minutes or until edges are lightly browned. Cool cookies on wire rack. Makes about 48 cookies.

Hickory Nut Cranberry Bread

An heirloom recipe from Grandma that you can bake and freeze ahead for holiday gifts.

Nonstick spray coating
3 cups all-purpose flour
1 cup sugar
4 teaspoons baking powder
1 1/2 teaspoons salt
1 1/2 cups coarsely chopped hickory
   nuts, divided

1 cup chopped fresh raw cranberries
1 beaten egg
1/4 cup soft shortening
1 1/4 cups milk
1 teaspoon vanilla

Preheat oven to 350°. Spray a 9 x 5 x 2 3/4–inch baking pan with nonstick spray coating and lightly flour. In a large mixing bowl, combine flour, sugar, baking powder, and salt. Stir in 1 1/4 cups of hickory nuts and cranberries. Blend well. Add egg, shortening, milk, and vanilla. Mix just until all ingredients are blended in. Pour into prepared baking pan. Sprinkle remaining nuts over top. Bake for 60 to 70 minutes. Let loaf stand in pan for 10 minutes, then turn out onto wire rack to cool. Makes 1 large loaf.

Apple 'n' Hickory Nut Pudding

This combination of hickory nuts and apples is a natural twosome for a fall dessert.

Nonstick spray coating
2 beaten eggs
1 cup sugar
1 teaspoon vanilla
1/3 cup all-purpose flour
1 tablespoon baking powder
1 teaspoon cinnamon

1/8 teaspoon salt
2 cups chopped, peeled apples
1/2 cup chopped hickory nuts
Unsweetened whipped cream, optional
Vanilla ice cream, optional

Preheat oven to 350°. Spray a 9 x 9 x 2-inch baking pan with nonstick spray coating. In a large mixing bowl, blend eggs, sugar, and vanilla until light and fluffy. Stir in flour, baking powder, cinnamon, and salt. Blend into cream mixture. Fold in apples and hickory nuts. Turn into prepared baking pan. Bake for 30 to 35 minutes or until apples are tender. Serve warm with unsweetened whipped cream or a scoop of vanilla ice cream, if desired. Makes 6 to 8 servings.

Rifles and Pancakes

Recipes in This Chapter

As October's bright blue skies gave way to November's windy chills, deer hunting became the main kitchen table topic. Once it began, Mother brought out Grandma Doughty's buckwheat pancake recipe so Dad could enjoy buckwheat pancakes just like the ones his mother made in her old-time deer hunting camp.

I'm talking about the old time, back in the woods deer hunting camp. The kind where deer stalkers pulled in a day early and didn't leave until the season ended nine days later.

The Doughty hunting camp off Highway 70 near Draper and Loretta was such a place. My grandparents operated it for nearly twenty years in the northern Wisconsin woods of Sawyer County. In its heyday, nearly sixty hunters gathered here during the late-November season.

A generation earlier, area lumber companies, such as Heinz, Paine and Chippewa Lumber & Boom, cut off the virgin hardwood timber. Before that, pine from northern Wisconsin rebuilt Chicago after the fire of 1871. In the pre-conservation days, lumber companies sold cutover land without replanting.

My grandfather, Harvey Doughty, coaxed a meager living on such cutover land. He cleared a few acres of stumps for crops. The marsh grass on the Thornapple River meadow furnished hay for his small herd of Brown Swiss cattle and four draft horses. He separated milk and shipped cream by rail to St. Paul. A flock of half-wild chickens kept the family in eggs. Wild berries and abundant game provided an ample diet, but income was short.

That is until Grandma thought of taking in deer hunters. Her idea became a family project. However it was Minnie Doughty who ruled the camp from her country kitchen in a small three-room house at the edge of the Thornapple meadow.

The men slept in a bunkhouse and several surrounding log cabins. Other hunters stayed at cabins miles back in the woods. They came two days before the season opened, sometimes when heavy snows blocked the old logging trails leading to their cabins. Grandpa hitched his team to a sleigh and hauled them in.

Grandma shook her head when told the amount of food they carried in. "More than their wives spend in a month on groceries," she said, "and before the season's over a good share will be up here eating."

She was right. Hunters might carry the food in, but that didn't make the meal. The optimistic cooks often didn't measure up. I remember one season when two hunters with a Milwaukee group appeared at the kitchen door.

"We hate to hurt Bill's feelings," one explained, "but we can't take his burned bacon and pork and beans another meal." The next evening they returned with two friends. The following evening the suspicious cook came storming into camp demanding to know what was going on. When they cautiously told him, he laughed and said, "Heck, you should have spoke up sooner. I can't stand that stuff either."

Grandma wearily pushed a few stray gray strands under a hairnet and shook her head. "As long as you're here, sit down and eat. Breakfast is at 5:30," she told them as they headed out the door. "Lunch is ready at noon, if you're interested. I only serve soup then, so don't expect much."

She kept me busy peeling potatoes, setting tables, and washing and drying dishes—which seemed a never-ending chore. When I asked about going up to the bunkhouse, I learned in no uncertain terms, it was off limits for me.

Groggy hunters yawned and stretched as they arrived for breakfast. Grasping steaming mugs of strong black coffee, they seated themselves on benches at the long table covered with a red-checked oilcloth. They came to at the sight of generous platters of buckwheat pancakes flanked by pitchers of maple syrup, bowls of fresh sour cream butter, pork sausage, and bacon.

Grandma started her sourdough buckwheat batter days before the season opened. Not one to fool with small batches, she used a ten-gallon earthen crock for mixing. She covered the crock with a white feed-sack dish towel to allow the fermenting yeasty batter to bubble and crackle its way to maturity. Each evening during hunting season, she relied on years of experience and a judgment call to feed the "seed."

I was still in grade school when she first trusted me to take charge of two oblong cast-iron pancake griddles at the wood stove. Each was large enough to make ten four-inch pancakes at once. Grandma handled three griddles on her range near the kitchen door. At the back of each stove, a coffee can held melted shortening and a flannel-wrapped fork to grease the griddles.

"Now, make sure the shortening dances on the griddle before you add batter," Grandma cautioned me. "I don't want any grease-soaked pancakes on my tables. Nor do I want them burned."

Only half-awake myself, I managed to follow her orders and before long pouring batter and turning pancakes became automatic. We handed platter after platter of buckwheat pancakes to the men at the table. They, in turn, handed a continuous flow of empty ones back for refilling.

I enjoyed helping serve the evening meal. I heard firsthand who hiked the farthest in the deepest snow, who sat at his stand the longest, who bagged a deer, whose buck had the most points, and who missed the largest one with a good shot. Never mind the teasing, the tall tales, the can-you-top-this bragging, or even the stacks and stacks of dirty dishes. It was exciting.

At the end of the season, the hunters lined up in the kitchen to settle their accounts. Armed with venison recipes and reservations for the next year, they headed out the door to return to their more sophisticated world with running water and comfortable mattresses. By the next morning, quiet returned to the camp and only tracks remained in the snow.

Although we didn't realize it until the late 1940s, the end loomed for the Doughty hunting camp and others like it. Motels and resorts opened their doors for the hunting season and the state's health department frowned on serving food to hunters in private homes. Then too, the deer moved south.

The Doughty camp is gone forever. The forest has reclaimed most of the homestead. Someone else owns the property now. However, I will never forget watching the hunters eating platter after platter of buckwheat pancakes, or listening to them swap hunting tales as they cleaned their rifles after dark.

Venison Meat Loaf

This recipe can be made with just venison. However the addition of pork makes a moist and tender loaf.

Nonstick spray coating	1/2 cup dry bread crumbs
1 pound ground venison	1/2 cup diced onion
1/2 pound ground pork	1/4 cup diced celery
1 beaten egg	1 1/2 teaspoons salt
1 cup milk	1/8 teaspoon pepper

Preheat oven to 350°. Spray a 9 x 5 x 3-inch loaf pan with nonstick spray coating. In a large mixing bowl, combine venison and pork. Mix well. In a small bowl, combine egg, milk, bread crumbs, onion, and celery. Mix thoroughly with meat mixture. Blend in salt and pepper. Spread evenly in prepared pan. Bake for 1 hour. Serve warm. Makes about 4 to 6 servings.

Venison Swiss Steak

You shouldn't have to conceal the flavor of venison. Preparing venison by the same methods that you use for beef of similar grade works just fine.

1/4 cup all-purpose flour	1 cup stewed tomatoes
1 teaspoon salt	2 large onions, chopped
1/8 teaspoon pepper	1/2 cup chopped celery
1 1/2 pounds venison steak, trimmed	2 tablespoons Worcestershire sauce
2 tablespoons shortening, or as needed	

In a small bowl, combine flour, salt, and pepper. Cut the venison into serving-size pieces. With a meat mallet, pound flour mixture into venison. In a large skillet, brown venison on both sides in hot shortening. Drain off excess shortening. Add tomatoes, onions, celery, and Worcestershire sauce. Lower heat. Cover and cook over low heat about 1 1/4 hours or until venison is tender. Remove venison to platter. Serve warm. Use drippings as gravy over mashed potatoes, hot rice, or noodles. Makes about 5 to 6 servings.

Roast Venison

Strong flavors concentrate in the fat, so trim cuts of venison before roasting. Overcooking can result in a dry and gamey flavor, so roast only to medium-rare for best results.

1 cup diced onion
2/3 cup salad oil
1/2 cup lemon juice
1 teaspoon salt

2–3 pounds boneless venison roast
3 slices bacon or salt pork
Horseradish, optional

In a small bowl, make a marinade by combining onion, salad oil, lemon juice, and salt. Mix thoroughly. In a large bowl, combine venison and marinade, turning the meat until well coated. Cover and refrigerate for 24 hours. The next day, preheat oven to 325°. Transfer and position venison in a Dutch oven with fatty side up. Cover meat with bacon slices. Roast for 1 1/2 to 2 hours (25 to 30 minutes per pound) or until meat is tender. Baste occasionally with marinade. If you are not sure if the meat is tender, cover while roasting. Serve on a hot platter with marinade and plenty of horseradish, if desired. Makes about 6 to 8 servings.

Venison Stew

Venison is likely to be drier and less tender than domestic meat, so moist heat cooking methods, such as stewing, braising, and pressure-cooking, are recommended. Venison's taste and texture are superb complements to the vegetables in this stew.

2 pounds of venison meat, cut in 2-inch pieces	1 bay leaf
1 clove garlic, minced	6 large carrots, cut in 1/2-inch rounds
3 tablespoons bacon fat	3 large onions, chopped
2 cups tomato juice	6 medium potatoes, cut in 2-inch pieces
Hot water, as needed	1 small head cabbage, cut into 8 wedges
1 teaspoon salt	
1/8 teaspoon pepper	

In a large Dutch oven, brown venison with garlic in bacon fat. Add tomato juice and enough hot water to cover venison. Add salt and pepper. Simmer, covered, over medium heat for 1 hour. Add bay leaf and carrots. Simmer for 30 minutes more. Add onions and potatoes. Continue to simmer for 20 to 30 minutes longer or until vegetables are tender. (You may have to add more water to keep ingredients covered.) Add cabbage and cover. Simmer for 15 to 20 minutes or until cabbage is tender. Remove bay leaf. Serve hot. Makes about 8 to 10 servings.

NOTE: Tough meats, especially from older animals, can be tenderized by basting with an acid such as orange juice. Besides giving the meat a delicate orange flavor, the acid in the juice helps to break down tissue and tenderizes the venison. Other acids include tomato, lemon or grapefruit juice, diluted vinegar, sour cream, pickle juice, and cooking wine.

Grandma D's Buckwheat Pancakes

Plan ahead to make these old-fashioned raised pancakes. The delicious results are well worth the effort—especially when served with warm maple syrup.

1 package active dry yeast
1/2 cup warm water
2 cups cold water
1 cup all-purpose flour
2 cups stone-ground buckwheat flour
1 teaspoon salt

4 tablespoons melted butter
1 tablespoon molasses
1 tablespoon sugar, optional
1 teaspoon baking soda dissolved in
  1/2 cup warm water

In a large mixing bowl, dissolve yeast in warm water. Add the cold water and blend. In a medium mixing bowl, combine all-purpose and buckwheat flours and salt. Stir to blend. Stir dry ingredients into yeast mixture. Beat vigorously until smooth. Cover tightly and place in refrigerator overnight. In the morning, stir butter, molasses, sugar and baking soda/hot water mixture into the chilled mixture. Let stand for 30 minutes. Heat a lightly greased griddle or heavy skillet over medium-high heat until a drop of water skates over the surface. For each pancake, pour 1/4 cup batter onto the hot griddle. Spread the batter out slightly to make a 4-inch pancake. Bake for 2 minutes or until bubbles appear on the surface and undersides are golden brown. Turn the pancakes and bake for 1 to 2 minutes longer to brown the second side. Serve the pancakes immediately or keep warm in a lightly covered ovenproof dish in a 200° oven. Makes about 32 pancakes.

Country Bean Soup

Truly a one-dish meal, this hearty soup is especially good during the winter months.

2 cups dried navy beans	1 cup diced potatoes
6 cups water	1 cup diced carrots
1 meaty ham bone	Salt, to taste
2 cups chopped onion	Pepper, to taste
1 cup chopped celery and leaves	2 tablespoons shortening
1 bay leaf	2 tablespoons all-purpose flour

Wash beans and drain. In a large heavy kettle, combine beans and water. Bring to boil over medium-high heat. Cook for 2 minutes. Remove from heat and let stand for 1 hour. Return to heat and add ham bone, onion, celery, and bay leaf. Cover and simmer for 2 hours or until beans are almost tender. Add potatoes, carrots, salt, and pepper. Cover and simmer for 30 to 40 minutes or until beans and vegetables are tender. Slightly mash vegetables with potato masher. Remove ham bone from broth. Cut meat from bone, dice, and return to broth. In a heavy skillet over medium heat, melt shortening and blend in flour, stirring constantly until mixture is thickened and smooth. Cook for 1 to 2 minutes to brown the flour. Gradually add 2 cups of soup broth, stirring constantly until the mixture is thickened and smooth. Add to soup broth to reheat. Makes 10 to 12 servings.

Thanksgiving on the Farm

Recipes in This Chapter

For our family, Thanksgiving and its traditions marked the beginning of the anticipated holiday season. Each year at the gathering of family, assorted relatives, and friends in our Wisconsin farm home, we bowed our heads and each in his own way gave solemn, thankful praise.

I don't mean to sound irreverent, but for my father a certain part of his "thankful" praise took on a whole different meaning.

You see, Mother had an unwritten rule. We couldn't open or eat any of her preserves and canned goods until every fresh item in the garden was gone. That generally meant Thanksgiving time.

We had a variety of fresh carrots, cabbage, parsnips, and rutabaga dishes until late fall. Dad complained about the same old routine, but Mother held off serving her winter's supply of preserves until she was certain winter had set in. "Just to make sure it will last," she kept repeating.

Let me tell you about Mother's fruit cellar. She believed in preserving anything and everything. Always a good canner, she "put up" more jars of produce in her time than most people. What she couldn't raise in her garden, we picked along the roadside or in the woods, or the neighbors gave us. Nothing went to waste. She started early in the spring with the fresh rhubarb. She first made sure we had our fill of the "spring tonic," then she canned and made rhubarb jam.

Even before school let out, she had

us out picking wild asparagus. Up and down the road we went. Father taught us how to snap the tender shoots, to get way down in the grass where the white parts nestled and not to miss any. The trick was to pick enough in one afternoon so Mother could can a kettleload of seven quarts after supper.

Our garden was often the first planted, first up, and first harvested in the neighborhood. We ate royally from it all summer. What we couldn't eat, Mother canned. And she canned all summer. I remember waking in the morning to find her in the kitchen with buckets and baskets of fresh vegetables, and seeing her still there when I headed to bed at night.

We ate fresh strawberries until we left some in the sauce dish. Then Mother made her jam and jellies. The raspberries, blueberries, and blackberries all worked the same. When Mother canned all she wanted and then some, Dad made wine with the rest.

Near the end of the growing season, the tomatoes, as if by magic, turned into sauce, juice, and stews. The cabbage was cut and cured into sauerkraut. Mother either canned the carrots or stored them in sand-filled milk cans. Pickles of every kind worked in crocks or sat on the shelves already canned. When the apple season started, we often found applesauce bubbling or apple butter simmering at the back of the wood range. About the time of frost, Mother paged through her Kerr and Ball canning books looking for different ways to put up a few remaining vegetables.

Still with all her canning, we didn't dare touch a pint or quart until we had to. Mother decided when we "had to." She kept us eating from the "rough" as long as possible. I am sure that there were times in late October and early November that our daily menus lacked something and we bordered on boredom and malnutrition.

Then, about the middle of November, Mother gave in and allowed us a jar of jam and some canned fruit for dessert. Finally, in time for Thanksgiving, she announced her fruit cellar officially open for the season.

We celebrated Thanksgiving with home-grown roasted rooster, the good old-fashioned kind with sage stuffing, squash, wild cranberry sauce, several kinds of canned vegetables, pickled beans, beets, sweet and sour pickles, pickled apples, and at least a relish or two. Our potatoes mashed up snowy white and rich with butter. We savored pies made from our own pumpkin, and enjoyed applesauce and blueberries picked under the hot summer sun. Mother opened several jars of her special blackberry and strawberry jam just for us to savor on her fresh-baked rolls.

Yes, we ate quite well on Thanksgiving. And once we started using the preserves and canned fruits and vegetables from the fruit cellar, Mother didn't mind a bit. We enjoyed balanced meals from then on.

So you can understand why we appreciated the coming of Thanksgiving at our home. I can still hear Dad exclaiming as he picked up his fork to take the first bite of his holiday dinner, "Thank goodness for Thanksgiving."

Country-Style Roast Chicken

A large, plump home-grown chicken, often weighing eight to ten pounds, starred as the featured delicacy at our Thanksgiving dinners. Sometimes, depending on the number of invited guests, Mother prepared two. Roasted to perfection, the golden-brown, juicy Thanksgiving chicken made a perfect centerpiece for an already overflowing table.

8–10 cups onion and sage stuffing, divided (see recipe, page 169)
1 6- to 7-pound roasting chicken, giblets removed and reserved for stuffing

1/2 teaspoon salt
1/2 teaspoon freshly ground black pepper
1/2 cup melted butter or margarine

Prepare onion and sage stuffing but do not stuff bird until just before roasting. Preheat oven to 325°. Rinse the chicken inside and out and pat dry with paper towels. Lightly sprinkle the inside of the bird with salt and pepper. Loosely spoon about 2 cups stuffing into the neck and body cavities of chicken. Do not pack. Bake the remaining stuffing separately. Tuck wing tips under the bird with neck skin under them. Place the bird, breast side up in a shallow roasting pan. Brush melted butter over the chicken. Roast the chicken, allowing 32 to 33 minutes per pound or until skin is crisp and chicken is cooked through. Baste chicken every 30 to 35 minutes during baking with pan drippings. Remove chicken from oven and let stand in warm place for 10 to 15 minutes before carving to allow juice to absorb. Makes about 10 to 12 servings.

Onion and Sage Stuffing

My mother learned to make this stuffing from her mother. Now five generations of our family are still enjoying it. It's mildly seasoned, so add more seasonings to your taste.

Nonstick spray coating
1/4 cup butter or margarine
1 1/2 cups chopped onions
1 cup chopped celery
2 teaspoons poultry seasoning
2 teaspoons ground sage
1 teaspoon ground thyme
1 teaspoon salt

1/4 teaspoon pepper
3 quarts slightly dry whole-wheat
   bread cubes
1/3 cup snipped parsley
Giblet and neck meats, diced
1 well-beaten egg
1-1 1/2 cups giblet broth (see recipe,
   page 170)

Spray a 2-quart casserole with nonstick spray coating. In a small skillet, melt butter over medium heat. Sauté onion and celery, stirring occasionally, until just crisp-tender. In a 4-quart bowl, combine onion mixture, poultry seasoning, sage, thyme, salt, and pepper. Mix well. Stir in bread cubes, parsley, giblet and neck meats, and egg. Mix well. Stir in 1 to 1 1/2 cups giblet broth, adding only enough to thoroughly moisten bread cubes without breaking them up. Reserve 2 to 2 1/2 cups of stuffing for the chicken. Spoon all the remaining stuffing into prepared casserole. Cover and refrigerate until baking time. Bake stuffing in same oven as chicken for 30 to 40 minutes. Baste the stuffing several times with pan juices from roasting chicken. Makes about 8 to 10 cups.

Giblet Broth

This was Mother's secret ingredient for delicious stuffing and gravy.

Chicken giblets
Chicken neck
5 cups water
1/2 cup chopped leafy celery tops
1 bay leaf
1 teaspoon salt

In a 3-quart saucepan, combine giblets, neck, water, celery tops, bay leaf, and salt. Bring to a boil over medium-high heat. Reduce heat. Cover and simmer 1 hour or until giblets are tender. Remove giblets and neck from broth. Chop meat fine. Refrigerate. Strain broth and refrigerate until needed for either stuffing or gravy. Makes about 4 cups.

Pineapple Cranberry Relish

The cranberries and pineapple create a tasty and colorful relish for holiday meals.

1 20-ounce can pineapple chunks
1/2 cup pineapple juice (reserved
    from can)
1/2 cup sugar
3 thin lemon slices
3 thin orange slices
1 stick cinnamon
2 cups fresh cranberries
1 cup chopped walnuts

Drain pineapple chunks and reserve juice. In a small saucepan, combine pineapple juice, sugar, lemon and orange slices, and cinnamon stick. Bring to simmering over medium heat and cook for 5 minutes. Add cranberries and simmer until they begin to pop. Add drained pineapple and nuts. Stir to blend mixture. Serve warm or cold. Makes about 4 cups.

Old-Fashioned Mixed Fruit Salad

This great make-ahead salad, patterned after the classic twenty-four-hour salad, is a holiday favorite.

1 29-ounce can fruit cocktail in light syrup, drained
2 11-ounce cans mandarin oranges, drained
1 20-ounce can pineapple chunks, drained
1 16-ounce can peach slices in light syrup, drained

3/4 cup chopped pecans
2 eggs
2 tablespoons sugar
1/4 cup light cream
3 tablespoons lemon juice
1 cup heavy cream, whipped

In a large bowl, combine fruit cocktail, mandarin oranges, pineapple chunks, peach slices, and pecans. Carefully mix. In a medium saucepan, beat eggs until light. Gradually add sugar, light cream, and lemon juice. Stir until well blended. Cook over medium heat, stirring constantly until thick and smooth. Cool to room temperature. Fold whipped cream into egg mixture. Pour over fruit mixture. Stir gently to coat all fruit. Transfer to serving bowl. Cover and refrigerate overnight. Makes 10 to 12 servings.

Acorn Squash with Cranberry Stuffing

Our family enjoyed winter squash baked plain and served with generous amounts of butter, cream, and a dash of salt and pepper. For special occasions, like Thanksgiving, Mother dressed it up a bit. The slightly sweet flavor of this squash lends itself to combining with fruit.

Nonstick spray coating
3 acorn squash
Water
2 tablespoons butter or margarine
1/4 teaspoon salt
1/2 teaspoon lemon juice

1 large apple, peeled, cored, and
    diced, about 1 1/2 cups
1 1/2 cups fresh cranberries
2 tablespoons water
1/4 cup sugar, or to taste

Preheat heat oven to 375°. Spray a large shallow, flat baking pan (large enough to comfortably hold squash halves) with nonstick spray coating. Wash and halve the squash; scoop out seeds and fibers. Place squash, cut side down in prepared baking pan. Add 1/2 inch water. Bake for 40 to 45 minutes or until squash is just tender. Meanwhile, in a medium saucepan, melt butter. Add salt, lemon juice, and apple. Cook over low heat until apple is tender. Add cranberries and 2 tablespoons water. Cook just until cranberries begin to pop. Add sugar. Stir until sugar is completely dissolved. Turn squash over in baking pan. Fill cavities with cranberry mixture. Cover and bake 15 minutes longer. Makes 6 servings.

Savory Creamed Onions

This tasty dish goes well with everything from roast poultry to beef and pork dishes.

2 pounds small yellow onions (larger than pearl onions)
Water
2 tablespoons butter
1 tablespoon all-purpose flour
1 cup half-and-half
1/2 teaspoon salt
1/2 teaspoon ground sage
1/8 teaspoon white pepper
1 teaspoon grated lemon peel, divided
1 teaspoon lemon juice
1 cup shredded cheddar cheese
1/2 cup chopped pecans
2 tablespoons chopped parsley
Paprika, for garnish

Preheat oven to 350°. Peel onions and cut thin slice from both ends. In a medium saucepan, bring water to boiling. Add onions, cover and boil gently for 20 to 25 minutes or until onions are tender. Do not overcook. Drain well. In a medium skillet, blend butter and flour. Stir in half-and-half, salt, sage, pepper, 1/2 teaspoon lemon peel, and lemon juice. Cook, stirring constantly, over medium-high heat until sauce boils and thickens. Remove from heat. Add cheese and stir until melted. Stir in pecans. Place cooked onions in shallow baking dish. Cover with sauce. Bake for 20 to 25 minutes or until heated through. Sprinkle with parsley, paprika, and remaining lemon peel. Makes about 5 to 6 servings.

Wild Rice Casserole

This casserole can be prepared a day ahead and baked just before serving.

Nonstick spray coating
1 cup uncooked wild rice, washed
   and well drained
3 3/4 cups chicken broth, divided
1 pound pork sausage
2 4-ounce cans mushrooms
1 medium onion, chopped

1/2 cup diced celery
3 tablespoons diced green pepper
1 clove garlic, minced
1/2 teaspoon salt
1/4 teaspoon pepper
1 cup slivered almonds

Preheat oven to 350°. Spray a 3-quart casserole with nonstick spray coating. In a heavy saucepan, combine wild rice and 3 cups chicken broth. Bring to a boil, reduce heat, and simmer, covered, 45 to 50 minutes or just until kernels puff open. Drain excess liquid and fluff with a fork. Meanwhile, in a medium skillet, sauté sausage, breaking it up into small pieces. Remove sausage from pan and drain on paper towels. Set aside. Pour off all but 2 tablespoons sausage drippings from skillet. Sauté mushrooms, onion, celery, green pepper, garlic, salt, and pepper in sausage drippings for about 5 minutes or until crisp-tender. Add almonds and cook for 1 minute. Combine rice and sausage with vegetable mixture. Add remaining broth and adjust seasoning to taste. Mix well. Pour into prepared casserole. Cover and bake for 30 minutes. Stir and continue to bake, uncovered, another 20 to 25 minutes to allow browning and remaining liquid to be absorbed. Serve warm. Makes about 8 to 10 servings.

NOTE: 1 cup of raw wild rice equals approximately 3 to 4 cups cooked wild rice.

Great-Grandma Doughty's Baked Beans

No one really remembers when Great-Grandma's baked beans—prepared in the old-fashioned gray earthenware casserole—first appeared on our holiday table. We only know that baked beans are as much a family tradition at Mother's Thanksgiving dinner as roast chicken.

4 cups Great Northern beans
Water
1/2 pound bacon, cut in 1-inch
  pieces
1 1/2 cups chopped onions, divided
1/2 cup packed brown sugar, divided

1/2 cup catsup, divided
2 teaspoons dry mustard, divided
2 teaspoons salt, divided
1/2 teaspoon pepper, divided
Hot water
Cider vinegar, optional

In a colander under running water, wash and sort beans. In a 4-to 5-quart kettle or Dutch oven, cover beans with water and let stand overnight. In the morning, drain. Preheat oven to 325°. Return beans to kettle and cover with fresh cold water and bring to a boil. Cook for 2 minutes. Drain, reserving liquid. In a heavy, well-greased earthenware casserole or bean pot, layer 1/2 of the beans, 1/2 of the bacon, 1/2 of the onions, 1/2 of the brown sugar, 1/2 of the catsup, 1/2 of the dry mustard, 1/2 of the salt, and 1/2 of the pepper. Add remaining beans and repeat layers of bacon, onions, brown sugar, dry mustard, salt, and pepper. Cover with reserved hot bean liquid, adding additional hot water if needed. Cover. Bake for 3 to 3 1/2 hours or until beans are tender and have absorbed most of the liquid, stirring once or twice. Do not allow beans to become dry. If beans show signs of drying out, add a small amount of additional hot water. To brown beans, remove cover the last 1/2 hour of baking. Serve warm with a splash of cider vinegar, if desired. Makes about 10 to 12 servings.

Cranberry Fruit Nut Loaf

You can use pecans, walnuts, hickory nuts, or any combination of nuts in this bread. Allow the bread to cool completely before slicing.

Nonstick spray coating
2 2/3 cups all-purpose flour
3 teaspoons baking powder
1 teaspoon baking soda
1 teaspoon salt
1/2 cup butter, softened
3/4 cup packed light brown sugar
2 slightly beaten eggs
1 cup small curd cottage cheese

1 cup (about 2 medium) mashed
   bananas
2 tablespoons grated orange peel
2 teaspoons grated lemon peel
2/3 cup orange juice
1 1/2 cups coarsely chopped
   cranberries
1 cup raisins
1 cup chopped pecans

Preheat oven to 325°. Spray two 8 x 4 x 2-inch loaf pans with nonstick spray coating and line with waxed paper. In a medium bowl, combine flour, baking powder, baking soda, and salt. Stir to blend. In a large bowl, cream butter and sugar until light and fluffy. Add eggs, cottage cheese, bananas, orange and lemon peels, and orange juice. Beat thoroughly until well blended. Gradually add flour mixture to cream mixture. Stir only until all flour is moistened. Stir in cranberries, raisins, and pecans. Divide batter between the two prepared loaf pans. Bake in for 65 to 70 minutes or until toothpick inserted in center comes out clean. Cool for 10 minutes. Remove from pans. Cool on wire racks before slicing. Makes 2 loaves.

Peanut Butter Pumpkin Pie

Everyone's favorite—peanut butter—blends nicely with pumpkin for a tasty variation on the traditional Thanksgiving pie.

Pastry for 9-inch single-crust pie (see recipe, page 37)	1/2 teaspoon ground cinnamon
3 eggs	1/2 teaspoon ground nutmeg
1 16-ounce can pumpkin	1/2 teaspoon ground ginger
1/2 cup packed light brown sugar	1/2 teaspoon ground allspice
1/2 cup granulated sugar	1/2 teaspoon salt
1/2 cup creamy peanut butter	1 cup light cream or half-and-half
	Whipped cream, for optional garnish

Preheat oven to 350°. Press pastry into a 9-inch, deep-dish pie plate or a ceramic quiche dish. Set aside. In a large bowl, beat eggs until well blended. Add pumpkin, sugars, peanut butter, cinnamon, nutmeg, ginger, allspice, and salt. Beat until light and fluffy. Gradually add light cream, beating until well blended. Pour into prepared crust. Bake for 65 to 70 minutes or until knife inserted in center comes out clean. To serve, garnish with whipped cream, if desired. Makes about 8 servings.

WINTER

Grandmother

Within her room she rocks and waits alone
She who a life of work and love has known,
And we who smile upon the gentle face
Can now but wonder at the inner grace
That stays her well with patience in these years.
We can but wonder if she sometimes hears
Beloved voices of another day.
Does she see loved ones here—and do they stay
Within her heart, and in this lonely room
Do forms and figures haunt the solitary gloom?
But when a shaft of sunlight filters through the trees
She nods in wonder, and we know she sees.
Is this enough, we ask, do memories compensate
(She's been so still and peaceful as of late)
Then through her window comes the call of an evening bird
We see her smile, and know that she has heard.

Anne M. Diley (1916–1969)

Christmas Baking

Recipes in This Chapter

Christmas came early to our country kitchen. It arrived with the teasing fragrance of holiday baking drifting through the house, then it went out the kitchen door in the form of festive fruitcakes, tins of Christmas cookies, and holiday breads.

Even before Thanksgiving dishes were dried and put away, Mother began planning her mincemeat, fruitcake, and cookie baking. She dusted off her heirloom recipe file and pulled out butter-stained newspaper clippings, recipe cards sticky with molasses, and the honey- and sugar-crusted notes from family and friends. She hunted up her green-handled cookie cutters and lined up baking supplies.

When I was in grade school, World War II was a factor in every event, even Christmas baking, because supplies were rationed or scarce. By managing our sugar allotment and using maple and corn syrup wherever possible, Mother saved enough for her baking.

For the next several weeks she spent all her time in the kitchen. The sweet scent of cinnamon, ginger, nutmeg, cloves, allspice, cardamom, peppermint, chocolate, molasses, vanilla, and almond combined with the flurry of holiday activity to fill our entire family with the Christmas spirit.

The day after Thanksgiving, Mother prepared a batch of spicy-sweet mincemeat and set the mixture aside in a crock to mellow.

"Good things take time," she told me.

Christmas baking officially began when Mother brought out the containers of sticky candied fruit, red and green candied cherries, dried fruit, nuts, and fragrant spices for fruitcake.

Mother believed in traditional fruitcake and enjoyed baking it, perhaps a bit more than we enjoyed eating it. Most of the time, it turned out heavy as lead, or as gummy and flavorless as the ones sold in the store. While we managed to slowly eat them, we did drop more than a few hints along the way. But she had a sense of humor, especially when a young hired man noticed her gathering fruitcake supplies.

"I always thought there was only one fruitcake in existence and it just keeps getting passed around every Christmas," he said.

"I'll pretend I didn't hear that," Mother replied. "Someone always brings up that old joke. This year I've made some adjustments and it's the best recipe I've found."

And she was right. We've been enjoying her special fruitcake recipe ever since.

With the mincemeat and fruitcake mellowing, an attack of cookie madness hit our country kitchen.

"Christmas wouldn't be Christmas without cookies," Mother insisted. Dad, with his sweet tooth, agreed.

Each day while I was in school, Mother stirred, mixed, and baked peanut butter balls, toffee bars, butterscotch creoles, jelly tarts, poppy seed cookies, red and green kaleidoscope crisps, and molasses-laced gingerbread cutouts. Best of all she made my favorites: buttery sugar cookies, in all sizes and shapes.

In the evening we sat around the table frosting and decorating what seemed like dishpans full of cookies. When we finished, a dazzling array of stars, bells, wreaths, trees, angels, and Santas lined the kitchen counter. Overnight, they disappeared into storage tins Mother lined up on the basement shelves next to the mincemeat and fruitcake.

There they sat until several days before Christmas when we brought them back up to the kitchen. Then the fun of packaging the holiday goodies into special containers to give to friends, neighbors, cousins, aunts, and uncles began. And best of all, each carried a message: "Merry Christmas from our country kitchen to yours."

Homemade Fruit 'n' Brandy Mincemeat

Good things take time. Mincemeat is not an impulse item unless you prefer the prepackaged style found on the grocer's shelf. Homemade mincemeat should be aged three weeks to a month before it is used.

3/4 pound fresh beef suet, finely
  chopped
4 1/2 cups apples, peeled, cored, and
  diced
4 cups raisins
2 cups dried currants
1 cup chopped walnuts
1 cup diced mixed candied fruit and
  peels
1/2 cup coarsely chopped dried figs
1/2 cup coarsely chopped dried
  apricots

1/2 cup coarsely chopped candied
  orange peel
1 1/4 cups sugar
1 teaspoon ground nutmeg
1 teaspoon ground allspice
1 teaspoon ground cinnamon
1/2 teaspoon ground cloves
2 1/2 cups brandy, plus more as
  needed during mellowing
1 cup dry red wine*, plus more as
  needed during mellowing

In a large bowl, combine suet, apples, raisins, currants, walnuts, mixed candied fruit, figs, apricots, candied orange peel, sugar, nutmeg, allspice, cinnamon, and cloves. Using a wooden spoon, stir the mixture until thoroughly mixed. Pour brandy and wine over all. Stir until well moistened. Pour mixture into a large container. (An earthenware crock works fine for this.) Cover and set mincemeat aside in a cool place (not in a refrigerator) for three weeks to a month. (Two months is even better). Check the mincemeat once a week. Do not let it dry out. As the liquid is absorbed by the fruit, replenish it with brandy and wine, using about 1/4 cup at a time. After mellowing mincemeat, pack in clean, dry containers and refrigerate or freeze until needed.

*For those who are purists: 1 cup of homemade dry red wine works fine.

Mincemeat Pie

Serve topped with vanilla ice cream for a special holiday treat.

Pastry for 2-crust 9-inch pie (see recipe, page 56)
3 cups homemade fruit 'n' brandy mincemeat

Preheat oven to 400°. Roll and fit pastry into 9-inch pie plate. Fill with mincemeat. Cover with top crust. Seal and flute edges. Bake for 35 to 40 minutes. Cool on wire rack. Makes 6 to 8 servings.

Mincemeat-Filled Cookies

These sweet-and-spicy treats are good with coffee.

3 cups all-purpose flour
1/2 teaspoon salt
1 cup butter or margarine, softened
1 cup sugar
1 slightly beaten egg

2 tablespoons milk
1 teaspoon vanilla
3/4 cup homemade fruit 'n' brandy
   mincemeat

Preheat oven to 350°. In a medium bowl, combine flour and salt. In a large mixing bowl, cream butter and sugar with an electric mixer. Scrape down sides of bowl as needed. Add egg, milk, and vanilla and beat until light and fluffy. Stir in flour mixture. Mix well. Roll dough out on a lightly floured surface to a 1/8-inch thickness. Cut with a 2-inch scalloped round cookie cutter. Re-roll as necessary. Place half of the cookies on ungreased cookie sheet. Spread about 1 teaspoon of mincemeat on each uncut round. Cut small holes in center of remaining cookies. Place on top of filling, sandwich fashion. Press edges to seal. Bake for 10 to 12 minutes or until edges are lightly browned. Cool on wire rack. Makes about 3 dozen cookies.

Very Best Fruitcake

Fruitcake's keeping power is remarkable. It can be wrapped in cheesecloth, soaked in the liquor of your choice, re-wrapped in foil and stored in an airtight container or the refrigerator for two to six weeks.

Nonstick spray coating
3/4 cup all-purpose flour
3/4 cup sugar
1 1/4 teaspoons baking powder
1/4 teaspoon salt
1 pound pitted dates
1/2 pound whole Brazil nuts

1/2 pound whole walnuts
1/4 pound candied cherries
2 well-beaten large eggs
1/2 teaspoon almond extract
Wine, brandy, or liquid of your choice,
    enough to moisten

Preheat oven to 325°. Line two 8 x 4 x 2-inch loaf pans with waxed paper. Spray paper with nonstick spray coating. In a small bowl, combine flour, sugar, baking powder, and salt. Stir to blend. In a large bowl, combine dates, Brazil nuts, walnuts, and cherries. Stir to mix. Sprinkle flour mixture over all. Add beaten eggs and almond extract. Using a wooden spoon, stir until all fruit is moistened. Spoon into prepared pans, pressing down firmly. Bake 1 to 1 1/4 hours or until a toothpick inserted in center of fruitcake comes out clean. Let cool in pan 10 minutes on a wire rack. Remove from pan and peel off waxed paper. Let cool completely. Wrap in cheesecloth, moisten with wine, brandy, or liquid of your choice, re-wrap in foil and store in an airtight container or the refrigerator at least 2 to 3 days to allow flavors to mellow. Check periodically to keep moist, adding 1/4 cup liquid as needed. Makes 2 fruitcakes.

Frosted Sugar Cookies

This recipe is a time-tested family favorite.

3 cups all-purpose flour
3 teaspoons baking powder
1 teaspoon salt
1/2 cup butter, softened
1 cup sugar
I well-beaten egg
1/2 cup milk

1 teaspoon vanilla
1 teaspoon almond extract
Warm milk for topping, optional
Colored sugars, optional
Ornamental butter frosting, optional
  (see recipe, page 186)
Nuts or candy sprinkles, optional

In a medium bowl, combine flour, baking powder, and salt. In a large mixing bowl, thoroughly cream butter and sugar. Add egg and beat well. Add flour mixture alternately with milk, vanilla, and almond extract. Stir until thoroughly combined. Dough will be sticky. Chill dough at least 2 hours or until stiff enough to easily handle. Meanwhile, preheat oven to 375°. Lightly grease cookie sheets. On a lightly floured surface, roll a small portion of the dough at a time to a 1/8-inch thickness. Cut into desired shapes with 2- or 3-inch cookie cutters. Place on prepared cookie sheets. If desired, lightly brush unbaked cookies with warm milk and sprinkle with a dusting of colored sugar. Bake for 10 to 12 minutes or until edges are firm and bottoms are lightly browned. Cool cookies on wire rack. If desired, frost cooled cookies with ornamental butter icing. Then sprinkle with nuts or sprinkles, if desired. To prevent sticking, spread the iced cookies in a single layer on a countertop for several hours or overnight to air-dry. Makes about 3 dozen cookies.

Ornamental Butter Frosting

Butter frosting made with large amounts of butter and little liquid remains moist for days.

4 tablespoons butter
$1/2$ teaspoon vanilla
Dash of salt
2 cups powdered sugar, divided
3 tablespoons orange juice, divided

In a medium mixing bowl, beat butter, vanilla, and salt with electric mixer on medium speed for 30 seconds. Slowly add $1/3$ of the powdered sugar, beating until well blended. Blend in 2 tablespoons of the orange juice. Gradually beat in remaining powdered sugar and enough orange juice to make frosting of spreading consistency. Makes frosting for 6 to 8 dozen cookies.

NOTE: Milk or cream may be substituted for orange juice in the above recipe.

Gingerbread Cookies

Nothing says Christmas like old-fashioned gingerbread cookies. One of their greatest charms is that they can be baked ahead. They keep well in the freezer or an airtight container.

3 1/2 cups all-purpose flour
1 teaspoon baking powder
1/2 teaspoon baking soda
1/2 teaspoon salt
1 teaspoon ground cinnamon
1 teaspoon ground ginger
1/2 teaspoon ground nutmeg
1/2 teaspoon ground cloves
1/2 cup butter or margarine, softened

1/2 cup packed brown sugar
1/2 cup molasses
1 slightly beaten egg
1/2 cup buttermilk
Raisins or currants, optional
Red cinnamon candies (Red Hots), optional
Ornamental butter frosting, optional (see recipe, page 186)

In a medium bowl, combine flour, baking powder, baking soda, salt, cinnamon, ginger, nutmeg, and cloves. Mix well. In a large mixing bowl, cream butter and brown sugar until light and fluffy. Add molasses and egg. Continue beating until well blended. Add flour mixture to cream mixture alternately with buttermilk, beginning and ending with flour mixture. Shape into a ball. Cover and chill for 2 hours or overnight. Preheat oven to 375°. Roll dough out to a 1/4-inch thickness on a lightly floured surface. Cut into desired shapes. Remove excess dough and re-roll. Place 2 inches apart on lightly greased cookie sheets. If using a gingerbread-man cutter, press several raisins or currents into each cookie for eyes, nose, and buttons. (For red buttons, press in red cinnamon candies instead of raisins.) Bake for 8 to 10 minutes. Cool on wire rack. Decorate with frosting and other ingredients, as desired. Makes about 3 dozen cookies, depending on size.

Poppy Seed Cookies

This dough keeps well in the refrigerator—just slice and bake as needed.

1 cup soft butter or margarine
1 cup sugar
1 slightly beaten egg
1 teaspoon vanilla
1 teaspoon ground ginger

1 1/2 cups finely crushed walnuts
1/2 cup poppy seeds
2 cups all-purpose flour
2 tablespoons sugar, optional

In a large mixing bowl, beat butter, 1 cup sugar, egg, vanilla, and ginger with an electric mixer on low speed for 30 seconds, scraping the bowl constantly. Beat for 2 minutes on medium speed, scraping the bowl occasionally. Add walnuts and poppy seeds. Beat on low speed for 1 minute. Gradually stir in flour. Mix well. Shape dough into 2 or 3 round logs. Wrap each log in waxed paper. Refrigerate at least 3 hours or overnight to chill well. Preheat oven to 325°. If desired, spread 2 tablespoons sugar on waxed paper. Roll logs in sugar to coat. Cut logs in 1/4-inch slices. Place 1 inch apart on ungreased cookie sheets. Bake for 15 to 20 minutes or until edges just start to brown. Remove from the baking sheet immediately. Cool on wire racks. Makes about 8 dozen cookies.

NOTE: Cookies may be stored in an airtight container at room temperature for up to 2 weeks or in freezer for up to 3 months.

Butterscotch Creoles

Don't be fooled by this rather plain looking refrigerator cookie. Rich and sweet, it is a perfect holiday treat to serve with coffee.

1 2/3 cups finely chopped dates
1/4 cup boiling water
3 cups all-purpose flour
1 teaspoon salt
1 teaspoon baking powder
1/2 teaspoon baking soda

2 cups packed brown sugar
1 cup butter or margarine, softened
2 well-beaten eggs
1 teaspoon vanilla
1 cup finely chopped walnuts

In a small bowl, combine dates and boiling water. Let stand 10 minutes to soften dates. In a small bowl, combine flour, salt, baking powder, and baking soda. In a large bowl, cream sugar and butter until light and fluffy, scraping down sides of bowl as needed. Beat in eggs and vanilla. Stir flour mixture into creamed mixture. Add dates and walnuts. Mix until thoroughly combined. Shape dough into 2 to 3 rolls. Wrap in waxed paper and chill for 4 to 24 hours. Preheat oven to 400°. Cut into 1/4-inch slices. Place on ungreased cookie sheets. Bake for 8 to 10 minutes or until golden brown. Cool cookies on wire rack. Makes about 100 cookies, depending on size.

NOTE: Use a long, sharp knife and a sawing motion to cut 1/8- to 1/4-inch-thick slices from chilled dough. Do not press too heavily on the knife. The thinner the slices, the crisper the cookies will be.

Date Sticks

These fruity bars are rolled in powdered sugar.

Nonstick spray coating
1 2/3 cups finely chopped dates
1/4 cup boiling water
1 cup all-purpose flour
1 teaspoon baking powder

1 cup sugar
1 tablespoon butter, softened
2 well-beaten eggs
1/2 cup finely chopped nuts
Powdered sugar

Preheat oven to 325°. Spray a 13 x 9 1/2 x 2-inch baking pan with nonstick spray coating. In a small bowl, combine dates and boiling water. Let stand 10 minutes to soften dates. In a small bowl, combine flour and baking powder. In a large mixing bowl, cream sugar, butter, and eggs until light and fluffy. Stir flour mixture into sugar mixture. Mix well. Stir in dates and nuts. Spread thinly in prepared pan. Bake for 18 to 20 minutes or until golden brown. Cool in pan. Cut into 3 x 1-inch strips and roll in powdered sugar. Makes about 3 1/3 dozen date strips.

Cherry Twinkles
A rich, nutty morsel capped with colorful candied cherries.

Nonstick spray coating
1 cup butter
1/2 cup packed brown sugar
1 slightly beaten egg
3 tablespoons warm milk
1 teaspoon vanilla
2 cups all-purpose flour

1/4 teaspoon salt
1 cup finely ground pecans
3/4 cup finely chopped candied
  cherries
Red and green candied cherries, for
  topping

Preheat oven to 400°. Spray a cookie sheet with nonstick spray coating. In a large mixing bowl, cream butter and sugar until light and fluffy. Beat in egg, milk, and vanilla. Mix well. Stir flour and salt into creamed mixture. Blend well. Stir in pecans and chopped candied cherries. Drop batter by teaspoonfuls onto prepared cookie sheet. Top with a piece of candied cherry. Bake for 8 to 10 minutes or until no imprint remains when touched lightly. Makes about 4 dozen cookie, depending on size.

Warm Starts for Icy Mornings

Recipes in This Chapter

Some folks claimed that our Morning Glory milk hauler (we'll call him Frank) had his finger on the pulse of his route. Others just called him a gossip, stating that he could circulate titillating tidbits from farm to farm faster than our ten-party telephone line. I remember Dad coming into breakfast at least once a week chuckling over the latest neighborhood scuttlebutt.

In the early 1950s I was still in high school, and breakfast was my responsibility; everyone else was up and in the barn by 4 A.M. for milking and other chores. Every morning, seven days a week, three hundred sixty-five days a year, they returned to the house promptly at 6:15 A.M. for hot cereal such as oatmeal, cornmeal, or farina. They also expected stacks of sour milk pancakes, sausage or fried cornmeal mush, potatoes, ham or bacon with eggs.

At some point, mid-milking, Mother returned to the house and called up the stairs, "Darlene, are you awake?"

Most times, she only called once and I was out of bed. A few times, depending on my social life, she called twice. That was all it took, because: (1) breakfast was my responsibility and (2) sleeping in was not tolerated—especially if I wanted to maintain an active social life.

In January of my senior year of high school, my social life in full swing, I continued to make the breakfast deadline.

However, there were a few close calls. Mother never said anything about it, but I detected an edge in her voice during those calls. While I suspected something was bound to happen, I had no idea the path it might take.

No doubt Mother came in that morning to call as she usually did. She claims I answered. Thinking all was well, she returned to the barn never realizing I'd fallen back to sleep.

At some point, my sleep-drugged mind registered the rumble of Frank's milk truck and the clatter of milk cans—the sounds I heard each morning while preparing breakfast. Reality hit when the sound of slamming truck doors vibrated into my dreams. Frank was at the milk house loading the milk cans. We needed milk for breakfast.

I bounded out of bed knowing there was no time to dress. Clutching my long flannel nightgown, I struggled to pull on my old purple chenille bathrobe. One shoulder seam hung loose. I pushed against it. Once. Twice. My arm finally found its way into a sleeve that hung by single thread. There wasn't time to hunt for the tie.

Looking under the bed for shoes, I only found worn felt slippers with leather soles. I jammed them on and headed down the stairs. In the kitchen, I grabbed the first kettle I could find and burst out the door.

Halfway to the milk house, I realized the new-fallen snow hid the icy patches on the uneven path. My leather-soled slippers found them and I started stumbling. Momentum carried me forward. My backside hit an embankment and, like a catapulting toboggan, I slid across the driveway toward the milk house. Just as I was about to crash against the building, Frank opened the door. Somehow he saw my tangle of arms, legs, flannel gown, and purple bathrobe coming straight at him.

Sheer instinct, or perhaps his guardian angel, flattened him against the door frame as I scooted past. I missed him by a fraction, but my troubles weren't over. The floor of the unheated milk house had its own sheen of ice and once I hit it, I spun and crashed against the concrete block wall under the wash tanks. Along the way I'd lost my kettle, a slipper, and a whole lot of dignity.

Frank, to his credit, never said a word. He silently helped me to my feet and found my slipper. While I put it on and shook my garments back into respectable order, he picked my kettle out of the snowbank and filled it with milk. Neither of us spoke when he handed it to me.

Drawing on all the royal decorum I could muster, I carefully returned to the house and my breakfast duties. There was no doubt in my mind that loud guffaws rang around the breakfast tables on the remainder of Frank's route that morning.

Beef Sausage Patties

A tasty, easy-to-make ground beef sausage that is excellent served with eggs or sour milk pancakes.

2 pounds lean ground beef	3/4 teaspoon pepper
2 teaspoons salt	1/2 teaspoon ground thyme
1 teaspoon ground sage	1 tablespoon butter

In a medium mixing bowl, combine ground beef, salt, sage, pepper, and thyme. Mix lightly but thoroughly. Divide and shape into 2 long rolls. Wrap in foil and chill overnight in refrigerator. (Roll can be saved in coldest spot of refrigerator for three days.) When ready to use cut 1/2-inch slices. Melt butter in a heavy skillet over medium-high heat. Add sausage patties and cook, turning to brown on both sides. Serve hot. Makes about 6 servings.

Sour Milk Pancakes

Besides being delicious, these classic, old-fashioned pancakes are quick to fix and tender, thanks to the sour milk.

2 cups all-purpose flour
1 tablespoon sugar
1 teaspoon baking soda
1 teaspoon baking powder
1/2 teaspoon salt

1 well-beaten egg
1 teaspoon vanilla
2 cups sour milk*
2 tablespoons melted butter or
    shortening

In a large mixing bowl, combine flour, sugar, baking soda, baking powder, and salt. In a small bowl, combine egg, vanilla, and sour milk. Mix well. Add to flour mixture and beat until free of lumps. Add and blend in butter. Heat a lightly greased griddle or heavy skillet over medium heat until a few drops of water dance across the surface. Pour sufficient batter on hot griddle to make a pancake of desired size (3 to 6 inches in diameter)**. Cook until full of bubbles and browned on under side. Then turn to brown on uncooked side. Turn only once. Makes about 2 dozen medium-sized pancakes.

NOTE: Sour milk can be made from sweet milk, by adding 2 tablespoons of white vinegar or lemon juice to 2 cups fresh milk. Allow to stand at room temperature for 1/2 hour, then refrigerate until using.

*If you like a sweeter-flavored pancake, add 1/2 teaspoon vanilla.
**If pancakes are too thick, thin with additional sour milk. If a thicker pancake is desired, add a little more flour.

Country-Style French Toast

It's hard to imagine that Mother's delicious homemade bread ever became leftover and stale, but from time to time it did. Rather than tossing it out, she made country-style French toast and served it with warm applesauce, maple syrup, and breakfast sausages. Everyone enjoyed this simple but special treat.

2 well-beaten eggs
2/3 cup whole milk
1 teaspoon vanilla

1/4 teaspoon salt
6–8 thick slices of day-old bread
6–8 tablespoons butter or margarine

In a shallow bowl, beat together eggs, milk, vanilla, and salt until well blended. Dip bread slices into egg mixture and soak them for a few minutes on each side, turning as needed to coat evenly but don't fully saturate. In a large heavy skillet, heat 1 tablespoon of butter over moderately high heat and cook batter-dipped bread until crisp and golden brown on both sides. Remove and keep warm. Repeat with remaining butter and bread slices. Serve warm with maple syrup and warm applesauce. Makes 4 to 6 servings.

NOTE: French toast, like pancakes, can be served with a variety of your favorite toppings such as honey, pancake syrups, assorted jams and jellies, or whipped cream and fresh fruit.

Homemade Brown Sugar Syrup

2 cups packed light brown sugar
1 cup boiling water
2 3-inch cinnamon sticks
1 teaspoon vanilla

In a medium saucepan, combine sugar and water. Bring to boiling, stirring until sugar dissolves. Add cinnamon sticks. Return to boiling. Lower heat and simmer for 10 minutes. Remove cinnamon sticks. Stir in vanilla. Serve hot or cold. Store in refrigerator. Makes about 2 cups.

Cornmeal Mush

Frigid winter mornings demanded hot cooked cereal for breakfast. We alternated serving cornmeal mush with oatmeal and farina.

    4 cups water
    1 teaspoon salt
    1 cup cornmeal
    Sugar, optional
    Cream, optional
    Melted butter, optional

In a medium saucepan over medium-high heat, bring the water to boil. Add the salt. Gradually beat in the cornmeal with a wire whisk or slotted spoon. Cook, stirring constantly, until thick and smooth. Lower heat. Cover and continue cooking for another 5 minutes. Serve at once with sugar and cream or melted butter and sugar. Makes about 4 to 5 cups.

Fried Cornmeal Mush

One of my father's favorite breakfast dishes from his childhood was fried cornmeal mush. He liked to pour maple syrup over the hot buttered slices served with eggs and sausage on the side. I liked it best with Mother's home-canned applesauce.

Prepare cornmeal mush as in the previous recipe or use any leftover mush from breakfast. Lightly butter a 9 x 5 x 3-inch loaf pan. Pour the cornmeal mush into the pan and smooth out the top. Cool to room temperature, then lightly cover with foil and refrigerate. When ready to cook, remove from pan and cut into 1/4-inch slices. In a heavy skillet, fry in bacon drippings or lard until brown on both sides. Serve with butter or margarine and maple syrup, applesauce, or tart jelly.

NOTE: For crisp-fried mush, dip each slice in dry cornmeal and use plenty of shortening for frying. Two cups mush makes about 4 servings.

Country-Style Fried Potatoes

Cold, leftover potatoes sliced paper-thin and fried in bacon drippings in a heavy cast-iron skillet make a mouthwatering breakfast dish.

1/4 pound bacon
6 cups thinly sliced cooked potatoes
2 tablespoons bacon drippings or shortening, or more as needed
1 teaspoon salt
1/4 teaspoon pepper

In a heavy cast-iron skillet, divide the bacon slices and fry until crisp. Remove the bacon and set aside. Pour off all but 2 tablespoons of drippings, saving the rest to use if needed. Layer the potatoes in the skillet. Fry the potatoes over medium-high heat, turning several times with a pancake turner, until they are browned and crusty on both sides. Add reserved bacon drippings as needed. Sprinkle with salt and pepper to taste. Serve hot with bacon on the side. Makes about 4 to 5 servings.

Breakfast Cocoa

Besides being delicious, a cup of steaming hot cocoa is always a welcome treat on frosty mornings.

2 tablespoons sugar
2 tablespoons cocoa
Few grains of salt
1 cup boiling water
3 cups milk
Few drops of vanilla

In a medium saucepan, combine sugar, cocoa, and salt. Gradually add boiling water to make a smooth paste. Bring to a boil over medium-high heat and cook for 5 minutes. Lower heat and stir in milk. Continue to cook for an additional 5 minutes longer. Beat a few minutes with a rotary eggbeater. Stir in vanilla. Serve hot. Makes about 4 cups.

Christmas Eve Supper

Recipes in This Chapter

Christmas Eve is my favorite night of the year. It has been since I was a child. But if ever excitement filled a country kitchen, Christmas Eve day was it.

As far back as my memory can take me, I remember the anticipation of invited guests and, of course, the tingling expectation of Santa's visit. Most of all, I remember the sights, sounds, and glorious aromas filling my mother's country kitchen. Cooking, baking, eating, and talking filled our day.

Traditions, traditions, and more traditions were what Christmas was all about.

For instance, I couldn't help feeling a bit smug when I told my friends at school that my family enjoyed not one but two Christmas Eve suppers. Our early supper was oyster stew and after midnight mass, we served Hungarian cabbage rolls and German stollen.

"It's our tradition," I proudly proclaimed.

Our day before Christmas started right after breakfast, when Mother brought in the big heads of cabbage and began preparing the Hungarian cabbage rolls. Years of practice made the job seem easy, but it was still time consuming. Once the heavenly aroma of the cooking cabbage rolls filled the kitchen, she began preparations for the next day's meal.

No matter where we lived, my parents invited company for Christmas dinner that often included grandparents, aunts, uncles, cousins, and many times friends, neighbors, and whoever else might be around for the holidays. Even though guests arrived with a dish to pass, Mother planned a complete menu.

"Just in case we have bad weather and they can't get here," she said.

She readied the turkey and sage dressing for the next day's roasting and set sweet dough for yet another batch of stollen. We peeled potatoes and set them aside in cold water. There was gelatin salad to ready; one batch of cranberries to cook for sauce and another ground for relish; pumpkin, mincemeat, and apple pies to be filled and baked; the giant Hubbard squash roasted along with Dad's favorite green bean casserole.

Midafternoon, my father appeared at the kitchen door and called, "Tree time!"

We rushed into the living room to clear a corner for the frosty, sharp-needled tree he dragged in. The Christmas tree, usually a balsam fir or spruce, was never quite perfect enough for Dad. He fussed, twisted, and turned it until he leaned back and announced, "That's the best I can do." With a resigned sigh, he left the tree to settle and unfold, and for Santa to trim on his Christmas rounds.

As with every other day of the year, farm chores demanded attention. The cows had to be milked at five o'clock each afternoon and again at five o'clock in the morning. Before Dad left the barn at night, he bedded the cattle with extra clean straw to ward off the cold Wisconsin weather and pushed fresh hay up in front of the cows.

I can still hear him telling us that at the stroke of midnight all the cattle in the barn could talk.

"How can that be?" we questioned.

"When Baby Jesus was born in their midst, he gave them the gift of speech in thanks for sharing their stable."

"Can we really hear them?

"Legend claims you can if you are there at the stroke of midnight," he assured me.

Whenever we heard that story, we vowed to go to the barn at midnight to hear what the cattle had to say. However, each year found us at midnight mass, so we missed hearing our cows talking.

On his way out the door, Dad tried to sneak a sample of the baked pie crust off the pumpkin pie, but Mother caught him.

"Drop that," she warned, "you know it's a fast day."

"It's just a little piece," he protested.

"Makes no difference."

In spite of all the food preparation going on in the kitchen, Mother held with the strict Catholic tradition of fasting the day before Christmas. That meant all our meals that day were slim and meatless.

Evening chores done, the men returned to the house for a light meal of oyster stew, crackers, and homemade bread. By the time we cleared the kitchen and covered the next day's food in the cold summer kitchen, bathed the little ones, wrapped last-minute family gifts and prepared gift boxes of cookies for friends at church, and arranged the crèche on a small table in the living room, it was time to get ready for church.

In my memory, Christmas Eve weather came in two distinct patterns. It was either a bitter cold night with a sky so filled with brilliant stars that you wanted to reach up and pluck one out of the Milky Way, or it was a world of gently fluttering snowflakes as big as the snowballs the grade school boys hurled at the girls.

"Christmas snow," my mother whispered. "Isn't it a lovely world of white? Just what Santa needs."

In the quiet hush of the late night, the choir voices rang out with the time-honored Christmas carols we all loved, including my favorite, "Silent Night."

By the time midnight mass was over, we rushed home and didn't hesitate to let Mother know we were starving. As we tumbled out of coats and boots, she brought in the kettle of cabbage rolls and began heating them.

Our sleepy eyes popped open as the rich aroma filled the room. We peeked into the living room to see if by chance Santa had paid an early visit. No such luck. Resigned, we returned to helping Mother put food on the table. She arranged slices of her rich German stollen, yule loaf, and cranberry bread on holiday trays and placed them in the center of the table. Then came a mouthwatering mosaic of Christmas cookies she'd kept out of our reach since baking them.

We savored the long-awaited cabbage rolls and devoured the breads and cookies, all the while proclaiming it all worth waiting for.

No matter how festive the meal became, Mother wasted no time in hustling us off to bed. Of course, we protested.

"How can Santa come if you're still awake?" she asked.

At 2:30 A.M., she had a point. From behind our bedroom door, we heard her moving about in the kitchen, clearing off our late Christmas Eve supper dishes. Then we heard other noises too, but sleep dulled our curiosity.

In the early morning, when we stumbled down the stairs, we found Santa had indeed arrived sometime before dawn and left a glittering tinsel-draped tree filled with opalescent balls. And wonder of wonders, a magical assortment of gifts surrounded the tree. A smiling nod from Dad set the day beginning in earnest.

It took us years to associate Mother's Christmas morning yawns and Dad's bleary eyes with Santa's wee-hours visit.

Hungarian Cabbage Rolls
(Toltott Kaposzta or tul-tot kah-poh-sta)

We are a versatile family and this is a versatile recipe in that, for as many cooks as we have in the family, no two recipes for Hungarian cabbage rolls are quite the same. However, we all agree on one thing: According to tradition, these rolls must be served at our after-midnight mass supper. The holiday breads and cookies are a perfect complement to this main dish.

1 large or 2 small heads of cabbage (at least 3 pounds) with fresh outer leaves
1 1/2 pounds lean ground beef
1 pound ground pork
2 cups cooked rice
2 medium onions, minced
2 tablespoons paprika
1 clove garlic, minced

1 egg
2 teaspoons salt, to taste
1/4 teaspoon pepper, to taste
3 cups sauerkraut with juice, divided
2 cups tomato juice, or more as needed
2 tablespoons shortening
2 tablespoons flour

Slice off the bottom of the cabbage head. Cut out as much of the center core as possible. In a large kettle, add enough water to fill 1/2 full. Bring to a boil over high heat. Drop the whole head into the boiling water and cook for 5 minutes, rotating to loosen leaves. Carefully peel off the outer leaves one by one. Lift them out of the water and drain. Stop when you get to the thick center leaves. Trim off the thick center vein of each leaf. You should have enough wilted leaves to make 15 to 20 cabbage rolls. In a large bowl, combine ground beef, pork, rice, onions, paprika, garlic, egg, salt, and pepper. Stir to blend well. Drain the water from the original large kettle. Layer 1/2 of the sauerkraut on the bottom of the kettle. On each cabbage leaf, place a large tablespoon of the filling in the center.* Roll up and tuck in the ends to make a neat package that won't come undone. (Do not make the roll too tight for the stuffing will expand in cooking.) Place the filled cabbage rolls in tight formation over the sauerkraut. Continue filling the leaves and layering them until the meat mixture is used. Shred any remaining cabbage and place over the rolls. Add the remaining sauerkraut and tomato juice over the top of the cabbage. Cover and simmer over low heat for 1 1/2 to 2 hours or until the cabbage is tender and filling is cooked.** In a heavy skillet, melt the shortening over medium-high heat and add the flour to make a roux. Brown it lightly, stirring constantly, then add several ladles of sauerkraut and tomato liquids. Thin it with 1 cup water. Cook for 3 to 4 minutes.

Continue stirring until the mixture is smooth and all lumps are removed. Pour over the cabbage rolls and bring the mixture to a boil. Serve from a deep bowl. Makes about 8 to 10 servings.

*The amount depends on the size of the cabbage leaf and the number of leaves you have.
**Check liquid often. Add more as needed or take some out if the mixture tends to boil over. Save any liquid you remove to add to the roux.

Traditional Oyster Stew

Thanks to my father's English heritage, rich and buttery oyster stew has become a Christmas Eve tradition at our family table.

1 quart oysters with liquid	1/2 teaspoon hot pepper sauce
1 teaspoon celery salt	Salt and pepper, to taste
1/2 teaspoon paprika	4–6 tablespoons butter
1 quart whole milk	Oyster crackers

In a medium saucepan, combine oysters and their liquid, celery salt, and paprika. Heat over low heat until edges of oysters curl. Add milk. Heat to serving temperature. Remove from heat. Stir in pepper sauce. Add salt and pepper to taste. Place 1 tablespoon butter in each soup bowl. Ladle in stew. Serve with oyster crackers. Makes about 4 to 6 servings.

Spicy Fruit Soup

A cross between a Scandinavian fruit soup and a German fruit compote, this dish can be served warm or chilled. Either way, clouds of sweetened whipped cream make a perfect topping.

1 1/2 cups chopped pitted prunes
1 1/2 cups chopped dried apples
1 cup diced dried apricots
1/2 cup diced dried pears
1/2 cup dark raisins
1/2 cup golden raisins
1 lemon, sliced and seeded
1/3 cup sugar, or to taste

4 cups water
4 cups apple juice
3 tablespoons quick-cooking tapioca
2 3-inch cinnamon sticks
6 whole cloves
Sweetened whipped cream for
   topping, optional

In a large Dutch oven, combine prunes, apples, apricots, pears, dark and golden raisins, lemon slices, sugar, water, apple juice, and tapioca. Place cinnamon sticks and cloves in a cheesecloth bag. Add to fruit mixture. Heat to boiling over medium-high heat. Cover and simmer for 30 to 40 minutes or until all fruits are tender but still firm. Remove lemon slices, cinnamon, and cloves. With a slotted spoon transfer the fruit to a heatproof bowl. At this point, taste to adjust sweetness. If more sugar is required, simmer several more minutes. Remove the pan from the heat and pour the syrup over the fruit. Serve the soup while it is still warm or refrigerate until chilled. Top with sweetened whipped cream, if desired. Makes about 8 to 10 servings.

NOTE: If you like, you may add 1/4 cup kirsch, brandy, rum, or white wine to the fruit along with the final addition of sugar.

Holiday Fruit and Nut Loaf

This is a wonderful holiday bread that can be baked ahead and frozen. We serve it thinly sliced with whipped butter.

Nonstick spray coating	1 beaten egg
1 package active dry yeast	1 cup uncooked rolled oats
1/2 cup lukewarm water	1 cup mixed candied fruit
1 cup milk, heated to 105° to 115°	3/4 cup chopped walnuts
1/4 cup sugar	Melted butter, optional
1/3 cup butter or margarine	Powdered sugar, optional
1 teaspoon salt	Powdered sugar glaze, optional
4-4 1/2 cups flour, divided	(see recipe, page 207)

Spray a large bowl with nonstick spray coating. Set aside. In a small bowl, soften yeast in lukewarm water. In a large mixing bowl combine milk, sugar, butter, and salt. Set aside to cool to lukewarm. Beat in 1 1/2 cups flour. Add and blend in egg and yeast. Stir in rolled oats, candied fruit, and walnuts. Stir in enough additional flour to make a soft dough. Turn out onto lightly floured surface and knead 10 minutes or until smooth and satiny. Place dough in prepared bowl, turning once to coat surface. Cover and let rise in warm place until doubled, about 1 1/2 hours. Meanwhile, lightly spray two 15 x 10 x 1-inch baking pans with nonstick spray coating. Punch dough down. Turn out onto a lightly floured surface. Let dough rest for 10 minutes. Shape dough into 2 round loaves. Place on prepared pans. Cover and let rise about 1 hour or until doubled. Preheat oven to 375°. Bake for 30 to 35 minutes or until lightly browned. Cool on wire racks. While still warm, if desired, brush top with melted butter, dust with powdered sugar, or frost with powdered sugar glaze. Makes 2 round loaves.

NOTE: If you plan to freeze the holiday fruit and nut loaf, do not frost.

Christmas Stollen

This traditional German Christmas stollen is both delicious and easy to make. If desired, whole red and green candied cherries can replace the assorted candied fruit. You can serve it warm, but it is even better if allowed to mellow for several days before thinly slicing it and serving with soft butter. An attractively wrapped Christmas stollen makes a lovely gift.

Nonstick spray coating
2 packages active dry yeast
1/2 cup lukewarm water
2 cups milk, heated to 105° to 115°
1/2 cup butter or margarine
1/2 cup sugar
2 teaspoons salt
2 beaten eggs
8–8 1/2 cups all-purpose flour, divided
1 1/2 cups assorted candied fruit and peels

1 cup chopped walnuts or pecans
1/2 teaspoon cinnamon, optional
1/2 teaspoon nutmeg, optional
Melted butter, as needed
Powdered sugar glaze (see recipe, page 207)
Whole red and green candied cherries, halved for garnish, optional

Spray a large bowl with nonstick spray coating. Set aside. In a small bowl, soften yeast in lukewarm water. In a large mixing bowl combine milk, butter, sugar, and salt. Cool to lukewarm. Add eggs and blend in 3 1/2 cups flour. Stir in yeast mixture. In a medium bowl, blend 1/2 cup flour with the candied fruit and nuts. Set aside. Add the rest of the flour to the dough, using just enough to make a firm dough. Turn out onto a lightly floured surface. Knead about 10 minutes or until dough is smooth and elastic. Place in prepared bowl. Brush with melted butter. Cover and let rise about 1 hour or until doubled. Spray 3 baking pans with nonstick spray coating and set aside. Punch dough down. Turn out onto a lightly floured surface. Divide the dough into 3 or 4 parts. Shape each part into a thick oval. Divide the fruit-nut mixture between each portion. Bring the edges together and begin lightly kneading to distribute the mixture evenly in the dough. Pat the dough into an oval about 10 inches long x 6 inches at the widest part. Paint each oval generously with melted butter and fold over lengthwise, bringing the upper half only about 2/3 of the way over so you have a traditional stollen shape. Press the edges down and brush again with melted butter. Place in prepared pans. Cover and let rise about 1 hour or until doubled. Preheat oven to 375°. Bake 10 minutes, then lower heat to 350° and continue baking for 25 to 30 minutes longer or until lightly browned. Cool on wire racks. While loaves are still warm, spread with powdered sugar glaze and decorate with halved red and green candied cherries, if desired. Makes 3 large or 4 medium Christmas stollen.

Powdered Sugar Glaze

1 cup powdered sugar
1/4 teaspoon almond extract
Milk, as needed

In a small bowl, combine powdered sugar, almond extract, and sufficient milk to make a spreadable consistency. Drizzle over still-warm Christmas stollen or use to frost the holiday fruit and nut loaf.

Cranberry Nut Bread

Cranberry and orange flavors team up to make a delicious holiday bread, especially when served—as we enjoy it—with softened butter or cream cheese. This bread must be cooled completely before slicing.

Nonstick spray coating
2 cups all-purpose flour
1 cup sugar
1 1/2 teaspoons baking powder
1 teaspoon salt
1/2 teaspoon baking soda
1/4 cup butter or margarine
1 teaspoon grated orange peel
3/4 cup orange juice
1 beaten egg
1 cup coarsely chopped fresh or
    frozen cranberries
1/2 cup chopped walnuts

Preheat oven to 350°. Spray a 9 x 5 x 3-inch loaf pan with nonstick spray coating and lightly flour. In a medium mixing bowl, combine flour, sugar, baking powder, salt, and baking soda. Cut in butter. In a small bowl, blend together orange peel, orange juice, and egg. Add to dry ingredients, mixing just until moistened. Fold in cranberries and walnuts. Turn into prepared pan. Bake for 60 minutes or until toothpick inserted in center comes out clean. Cool on wire racks for 10 minutes. Remove from pan. When completely cool, wrap and store overnight or freeze. Makes l loaf.

Drop-In Company

Recipes in This Chapter

In January, when winter sent north winds howling, leaving snowdrifts higher than our shoulders, life slowed considerably. Once we returned to school after Christmas vacation, Mother wasted no time removing the tinsel and holiday lights from the Christmas tree. She ignored our protests when we came home after school to find the living room corner empty and all the signs of the holiday packed away for another year.

As life became routine, the winter doldrums set in. The men fed the cattle, cleaned up after them and milked twice a day. Between chore times, in spite of a heavy blanket of snow, they went to the woods to cut trees for the following year's cooking and heating.

Mother, in turn, kept busy with the never-ending household chores. Any spare time she found, she picked up her crochet hook and thread to turn into gifts for relatives and friends.

Looking back on what I thought of as a quiet time, I now realize Mother was also busy keeping the kitchen fragrant with her baking. She especially enjoyed making a wide variety of cakes—always from scratch—and always managed to have a couple on the pantry shelf.

Her angel food cakes were light, delicate, and majestic creations she saved for Sunday dinner and special occasions like church suppers. What she called her "everyday cakes," such as chocolate chip prune, poppy seed with lemon topping, hickory nut and cherry upside-down cake among others, all earned hearty applause in the neighborhood.

"Never know who might drop in," she said to explain the spicy aroma drifting about her cheery kitchen.

Dad agreed she had a point. Back in the early 1940s before we had a telephone, drop-in company was an accepted part of our lifestyle. That term did not refer to the salesmen, deliverymen, or neighbors who called on business during the week.

What drop-in company really meant was any relative, neighbor, or friend who knocked on our back door (only strangers came to the front door) and said, "Just driving by and thought we'd drop in and say 'Hello.'"

"Course we're home," Dad always said. He waved them and called over his shoulder, "Put the coffee on. We've got company."

At times, older folks with no children dropped in for a visit on Sunday afternoons. On other occasions, entire families came to call. The Taylors were such a family. Adventurous souls, they dared to travel the frigid snow-covered winter roads on Sunday evenings. This meant all eight Taylor children, from baby Grace to fifteen-year-old Philip, came visiting with their parents.

After they all stomped the snow off their shoes and stripped off their coats, everyone milled around generally making themselves at home. Gradually the women laid the little ones down to sleep on my parents' bed and settled in the dining room to compare notes and recipes. The men and older boys clustered around the kitchen table to play cards and visit. At some point, they donned their jackets and headed for the barn to look at the cows or pigs or horses.

Meanwhile, that left six-year-old Norma, who was in first grade with me at the local one-room school, her four-year-old brother Lawrence, and the second-grade twins, Ruben and Myron, free to entertain ourselves. Or more to the point, get into trouble—something we always managed to do.

It often involved some innocent-sounding (at least to us) game that quickly escalated into a noisy game with name calling and a war of words that sounded just like the ones my father used when the cows broke out.

Mother caught my eye and pointed to the chair beside her. "Sit."

I think Mrs. Taylor finally recognized the desperate tone in Mother's voice, because she lined up her brood on the sofa with a stern, "Knock it off."

As I recall, calm lasted less than three minutes before someone wiggled. The chain reaction led to a nudge that became a push followed by a shove and back down the line. A giggle became a protest that led to a burst of tears from the older trio's little brother.

That caught Mrs. Taylor's attention.

"I didn't do anything, Ma," Ruben protested. "He started it." Myron nodded in agreement.

Mother jumped up and grabbed my arm. "Time to put the coffee on." Tugging me along to the kitchen, she never gave me the chance to see which one of the four Mrs. Taylor cuffed.

A cup of warm cocoa along with a generous piece of Mother's applesauce carrot cake dried the youngster's tears and subdued his restless siblings. When she offered them a piece of chocolate chip prune cake eager hands held out their plates.

Later, we stood in the doorway and watched all ten of the Taylors jostle into their '38 Chevrolet. My father shook his head and said, "They're packed in like sardines."

I heard his consoling whisper when he placed his arms around Mother's shoulders. "Maybe the next time they drop in it will be summer and the kids can play outdoors."

Applesauce Carrot Cake

Raisins, nuts, and a blend of spices added to the combination of applesauce and carrots make this a family favorite.

Nonstick spray coating
2 3/4 cups all-purpose flour
3 teaspoons baking soda
1 teaspoon salt
3 teaspoons cinnamon
1 teaspoon nutmeg
4 eggs, slightly beaten

3/4 cup cooking oil
2 cups sugar
1 teaspoon vanilla
1 15-ounce can applesauce
3 cups shredded carrots
1 cup raisins
1 cup chopped walnuts, divided*

Preheat oven to 350°. Spray a 13 x 9 x 2-inch baking pan with nonstick spray coating. In a mixing bowl, combine flour, baking soda, salt, cinnamon, and nutmeg. Set aside. In a large mixing bowl, combine eggs, cooking oil, sugar, and vanilla. Beat until well combined. Add applesauce and carrots. Stir until well blended. Add flour mixture to applesauce mixture, stirring just to moisten. Fold in raisins and 1/2 cup walnuts. Pour batter into prepared baking pan. Sprinkle with remaining walnuts. Bake for about 45 minutes or until a toothpick inserted in center comes out clean. Cool on wire rack. Makes about 12 servings.

*This cake can be varied by adding all the walnuts into the cake batter before baking and then frosting the cake with a butter frosting (see recipe, page 66) after cooling.

Butter Frosting

4 tablespoons butter or margarine
1 teaspoon vanilla
2 cups powdered sugar
3 tablespoons milk

In a medium mixing bowl, combine butter and vanilla. Beat until butter is softened and fluffy. Gradually add powdered sugar and 1 to 2 tablespoons of milk at a time, beating well after each addition. Beat in additional milk, if necessary, to make spreading consistency. Makes enough to frost a 13 x 9 x 2-inch cake or two 8- or 9-inch cakes.

Jellyroll

We all enjoyed jellyrolls, especially Mother. She claimed it was one of the simplest desserts to prepare because it can be whipped up quickly, baked for just a few minutes, rolled, unrolled, and filled with a variety of jellies or jams. A jellyroll makes a perfect late-evening snack when paired with a pot of fresh-brewed coffee.

Nonstick spray coating
1 cup all-purpose flour
1 teaspoon baking powder
1/4 teaspoon salt
4 eggs
3/4 cup granulated sugar
1/3 cup water

1 teaspoon vanilla
1/4 teaspoon almond extract
Powdered sugar, as needed
2/3 cup tart jelly or jam, such as
    cherry, current, plum or your
    favorite flavor
Powdered sugar

Preheat oven to 350°. Lightly spray a 15 1/2 x 10 1/2 x 1-inch jellyroll pan with nonstick spray coating. Line the bottom of the pan with waxed paper and lightly spray the paper. In a small mixing bowl, combine flour, baking powder, and salt. In a large mixing bowl, beat eggs with an electric mixer until fluffy and thickened. Gradually add granulated sugar, beating constantly until the mixture is very thick and lemon-colored. Reduce the mixer speed to low and beat in water, vanilla, and almond extract. Sprinkle flour mixture over egg mixture. Fold in gently, just until moistened. Spread evenly in prepared pan. Bake for 12 to 15 minutes or until center springs back when lightly pressed with fingertip. Immediately loosen edges of cake from the pan. While still warm, carefully turn out onto a clean dish towel sprinkled with powdered sugar. Remove pan and waxed paper. Starting with the narrow end, roll up warm cake and towel together. Cool completely on a wire rack. When cake is cool, unroll. Remove towel. Lightly sprinkle cake with powdered sugar. In a small bowl, beat jelly or jam slightly with a fork to soften. Using a dinner knife, spread jelly or jam evenly over the entire surface of the cake. Re-roll without the towel. Chill several hours or overnight. To serve, cut into 1-inch slices with a serrated knife. Makes about 10 servings.

NOTE: A jellyroll must be rolled while it is still warm to prevent it from cracking.

Poppy Seed Cake

This cake is tender, moist, and speckled with crunchy poppy seeds that play wonderfully against the tart lemon pudding topping spooned over the top.

Nonstick spray coating	1 1/2 cups sugar
1/3 cup poppy seeds	1 cup water
1/2 cup water	4 egg whites, stiffly beaten
2 cups all-purpose flour	Lemon pudding topping (see recipe below)
2 teaspoons baking powder	Sifted powdered sugar, for optional garnish
1/2 teaspoon salt	
3/4 cup butter or margarine	

Soak poppy seeds in 1/2 cup water for 2 hours. Drain off water. Preheat oven to 350°. Spray a 13 x 9 x 2-inch baking pan with nonstick spray coating and lightly flour. In a small bowl, combine flour, baking powder, and salt. In a large mixing bowl, combine butter and sugar and beat with electric mixer on medium speed until light and fluffy. Add poppy seeds and continue beating until well blended. Gradually add flour mixture alternately with the 1 cup water to creamed mixture. Fold in beaten egg whites. Pour into prepared baking pan. Bake for about 30 minutes or until toothpick inserted in center comes out clean. Cool completely on wire rack. Spread lemon pudding topping over the cake and dust with powdered sugar, if desired. Makes about 12 servings.

Lemon Pudding Topping

4 egg yolks	1 tablespoon butter or margarine
1/2 cup sugar	4 tablespoons lemon juice
6 teaspoons cornstarch	2 tablespoons finely shredded lemon peel
1 cup cold water	

In a small mixing bowl, beat egg yolks with an electric mixer until thick and lemon-colored. In a medium saucepan, combine sugar and cornstarch. Stir in water and beaten egg yolks. Cook and stir over medium heat until bubbly. Continue cooking and stirring for an additional 2 minutes. Remove from heat. Stir in butter, lemon juice, and lemon peel. Cover with plastic wrap and chill well. Makes about 2 cups.

Salted Peanut Cake

This winning combination had everyone asking for seconds. Mother ground her peanuts under a rolling pin or with a food grinder, but a blender works even better.

Nonstick spray coating	1 cup sugar
1 1/2 cups all-purpose flour	1/2 cup butter or margarine, softened
1 teaspoon baking soda	2 eggs
1/8 teaspoon salt	1 cup buttermilk or sour milk
1 cup finely ground Spanish peanuts	Caramel frosting (see recipe, below)

Preheat oven to 350°. Spray a 13 x 9 x 2-inch cake pan with nonstick spray coating. In a small bowl, combine flour, baking soda, and salt. Blend in ground peanuts. In a large mixing bowl, cream sugar and butter until light and fluffy. Add eggs, one at a time, beating thoroughly after each addition. Add flour mixture to egg mixture alternately with milk, stirring only until moistened. Pour into prepared pan. Bake for 35 minutes or until toothpick inserted near center comes out clean. Cool on wire rack. Frost with caramel frosting in pan. Makes about 12 servings.

Caramel Frosting

2 cups packed brown sugar
1/2 cup milk
1/2 cup butter or margarine
1/4 teaspoon salt
1 teaspoon vanilla

In a medium saucepan, combine sugar, milk, butter, and salt. Cook and stir over medium heat until butter is melted. Bring to a full rolling boil, stirring constantly. Boil 1 minute. Remove from heat. Beat with an electric mixer until lukewarm. Stir in vanilla. Continue beating at high speed until frosting has smooth spreading consistency. Spread on cooled cake. Makes enough to frost a 13 x 9 x 2-inch cake or an 8- or 9-inch 2-layer cake.

Chocolate Chip Prune Cake

The tasty prune tidbits lend the moisture while the crown of chocolate chips, sprinkle of brown sugar, and the scattering of chopped walnuts combine to make a perfect cake to have on hand to serve warm or cold to drop-in company.

Nonstick spray coating
1 cup finely chopped pitted prunes
1 scant teaspoon baking soda
1 1/4 cups boiling water
3/4 cup butter or butter-flavored shortening
1 cup granulated sugar

2 eggs, slightly beaten
2 cups all-purpose flour
1 teaspoon baking powder
1 teaspoon salt
1 cup chocolate chips
1/2 cup packed brown sugar
1/2 cup chopped walnuts

Preheat oven to 350°. Spray a 13 x 9 x 2-inch baking pan with nonstick spray coating. In a small bowl, combine prunes and baking soda with boiling water. Stir to completely cover prunes. Set aside. In a large mixing bowl, cream together butter, granulated sugar, and eggs until light and fluffy. Add the prune mixture and beat until well combined. Add the flour, baking powder, and salt. Stir mixture just until moistened. (Batter will be thick.) Pour mixture into prepared baking pan. In a small bowl, combine chocolate chips, brown sugar, and walnuts. Sprinkle over batter. Bake for 40 minutes or until a toothpick inserted near the center comes out clean. Cool cake in pan on wire rack. Makes about 16 servings.

Sloppy Joes

Mother often served sloppy joes, her favorite home-style fast food, to drop-in company. My guess is that every one of her friends had their own recipe for this hot sandwich. Although the name varied—some served barbecues while others served chili burgers, saucy joes, or spoon burgers—the recipe was basically the same: ground beef, a zesty tomato sauce (such as stewed tomatoes, catsup, or, in some cases, tomato soup), chopped onions, celery, and a touch of spices. Mother served her sloppy joes on homemade buns or bread.

2 pounds ground beef
1 1/2 cups finely chopped celery
1 1/2 cups finely chopped onions
1 tablespoon Worcestershire sauce
2 teaspoons paprika

1 teaspoon salt
1/4 teaspoon pepper
1/4 teaspoon garlic powder, or to taste
2 cups stewed tomatoes

In a large skillet, crumble and brown ground beef over medium heat. Add celery and onions. Stir to blend. Continue browning the mixture until the celery and onions are tender. Stir in Worcestershire sauce, paprika, salt, pepper, and garlic powder. Add stewed tomatoes, stirring until well mixed. Lower heat and simmer for 30 to 35 minutes, stirring often to blend flavors and thicken. Makes about 12 servings.

Neighborhood Butchering Bee

Recipes in This Chapter

When I was growing up, meat was the main item in our diet. No meal was complete without it. Since my father and brothers enjoyed hunting and fishing, we ate a lot of wild game, including venison, rabbit, squirrel, pheasant, grouse, and a variety of fish. However, our daily diet mainly revolved around poultry, beef, and pork—all farm raised and butchered.

For some reason I never quite figured out, no matter where we lived, my father was the neighborhood butcher. He not only provided the site for the butchering bee and engineered the process, he also helped with the meat cutting afterward and the grinding of the meat for sausage and lard. The neighborhood looked to him to help with the curing and hickory smoking of the bacons and hams. However, he drew the line at rendering the lard. That was Mother's job.

Preparations for butchering began when the weather turned crisp and cold after a January thaw. The neighbors arrived with their animals the day before the planned butchering day. Once they unloaded them into a special pen, the men began to prepare the butchering site. While some gathered equipment, others arranged a hoist and scraping table against which the wooden scalding barrel tilted at a 45-degree angle. It took several strong men to position the large logs into a tripod to hold the big black cast-iron kettle over a fire pit. Several other men gathered and chopped firewood.

The next morning, before sunup, Dad filled the kettle with water and built a crackling fire. By the time the water began to boil, men and women from the neighborhood had pulled into the yard. The scene quickly turned into an assembly line as each man hustled to his assigned chore. The women joined Mother in the kitchen.

Several days before Mother had baked bread and several batches of molasses cookies and brownies to serve to the workers. She always prepared a big kettle of chili for lunch on those frosty January butchering days. Her recipe certainly wasn't fancy. In fact, she carried it in her head and passed it along orally to anyone who asked.

"All it is," she said with a shrug, "is ground beef, kidney beans, onions, celery, elbow macaroni, my home-canned tomatoes, and some seasonings."

The seasonings! That's what made her chili so special. She never measured, just poured some in the palm of her hand and sprinkled it in. Her choice of seasonings and methods of measuring certainly turned out a terrific chili that earned her a faithful following.

That is until the butchering day she ran out of chili powder. That morning I'd browned the meat, onions, celery, and added all the other ingredients except for the seasonings. That was her job.

I turned from washing dishes when I heard her mumbling over the chili kettle.

"I ran out of chili powder," she whispered in answer to my question. In desperation we checked the cupboards several times, but only came up with cayenne pepper. It only took a second for her to make up her mind and grab the container from me.

As she held the open cayenne pepper can over the bubbling chili, the kitchen door slammed open, followed by the clatter of empty dishpans rolling into the room. We spun around to see Mother's friend Marie with an apologetic look on her face.

"Frost on the steps," she explained.

When Mother's attention returned to the chili, she gasped in horror at the colossal blotch of cayenne pepper slowly sinking into the gurgling tomato mixture. Before she found a spoon to scoop some out, the last of the pepper disappeared.

"Guess no one will miss the chili powder," she said with a sigh and added more tomatoes and water to the broth.

Once she left the covered chili pot simmering on the old wood range, Mother turned her attention to the mounting activity around her.

As the dishpans filled with organ meat brought into the kitchen, the women washed the tongues, cleaned and stripped veins from the hearts, livers, and kidneys. When they finished each batch, they placed everything in salted water in scoured galvanized washtubs to cool in the frigid summer kitchen.

Several hours later, when the men came into lunch, they commented on the wonderful aroma in the kitchen. As soon as we placed the steaming bowls before them, I noticed that the first to sample the chili began to gulp and cough. Then another tried to cover a choking sound.

Mother took one look at the men's faces and went for water. She tried to apologize for the chili's intense heat, but the men brushed her words aside.

"It's got personality," one man insisted as he wiped the sweat from his brow. Several others gulping water nodded in agreement.

"You guys are a bunch of sissies," a loyal fan of Mother's chili piped up. "A little fire in the belly is what we need when it's below zero outside."

I noticed he was the only one to ask for a second bowl of chili.

At the end of the day 10 to 15 headless hogs hung upside down to chill overnight on the poles braced between the open machine-shed doors.

Supper on the first day of butchering always featured fresh pork liver dipped in seasoned flour, then quickly fried in bacon grease, and smothered in onions in a hot cast-iron skillet. Fresh pork liver has a mild, delicate flavor that lasts only a short time before changing into a completely different taste. Mother always prepared generous platters of the annual treat.

The hustle and bustle of kitchen activity continued the following days and nights. The meat needed immediate attention before it spoiled.

Our antique kitchen table still bears marks from when my father used his meat saw to cut and trim the pork carcass into usable portions. Using a sharp knife, he separated the future ribs, hams, and bacons and set them aside for curing and hickory smoking in the small smokehouse behind the woodshed. As he continued cutting roasts, steaks, and chops, Mother wrapped the meat for freezing.

Two giant washtubs sat on the floor next to the table. Into one went the fatty scraps for rendering. The other held the trimming scraps scheduled for sausage.

Once he finished cutting up the carcasses, Dad set up the heavy-duty meat grinder locked into position on a thick board resting between two chairs. He turned the cumbersome crank by hand while I fed the scraps into the grinder. The task completed, he seasoned the meat with salt, pepper, sage, and assorted seasonings. Finally he stuffed the blended mixture into cleaned hog casings and set them aside for smoking.

Other pork odds and ends—snouts, ears, skins, and bits of meat—were boiled with spices, deboned, diced, or ground. Mother placed the resulting mixture into a cheesecloth bag and pressed it into loaf bread pans. Placing them on a table in the summer kitchen, she left the mixture to jell into head cheese.

By the end of the week, all the meat was in the freezer, the hams and bacons were curing, and the sausages were smoking over a slow hickory fire. Mother finished rendering the lard and stored it in heavy earthenware crocks on basement shelves. And Dad had the pigs feet cleaned and ready for our favorite Hungarian meal of kocsonya.

Homemade Pork Sausage

If you are a sausage fan, you may enjoy making your own country bulk-type sausage. It contains less fat, it's flavored to your taste, and it's as easy as you want to make it. This is a fresh sausage, the kind you use for patties, meatballs, spaghetti sauce, and chili or as a pizza topper. To make this homemade sausage more definitively your own, you might begin by choosing herbs like thyme, marjoram, sage, and fennel.

2 pounds boneless pork shoulder, cut into small pieces
2 teaspoons salt
1 1/2 teaspoons dried sage, crushed
3/4 teaspoon paprika

1/4 teaspoon ground allspice
1/4 teaspoon fennel seed
1/4 teaspoon garlic powder
1/4 teaspoon black pepper

Grind pork with coarse blade of meat grinder. Stir in salt, sage, paprika, allspice, fennel seed, garlic powder, and pepper. Mix well. Using fine blade, grind mixture again. Shape into two rolls. (Or shape into 1/2-inch thick patties.) Wrap tightly with foil. Chill in the refrigerator 24 hours, allowing flavors to develop. Makes 2 pounds sausage.

NOTES: To cook sausage patties: Start them in a cold skillet over medium heat. Cook until well done and brown on both sides. Or place the patties on an unheated rack in a shallow baking pan and bake at 400° for about 20 minutes or until done.

Keep in mind that fresh sausage is highly perishable. If you don't plan to use it within 2 days, it's best to freeze it.

Beat-off-the-Chill Chili

One great thing about chili is that it's easy to improvise according to what you have on hand and what your family likes best. There are almost as many ways to season chili as there are people to eat it. This is Mother's version. Feel free to make your own adjustments to seasoning amounts. Keep in mind that chili flavor always improves if it is left to develop overnight.

1 1/2 pounds lean ground beef
1 cup chopped celery
1 cup diced onion
1 clove garlic, minced
3 tablespoons chili powder
2 tablespoons Worcestershire sauce
2 teaspoons paprika
1 teaspoon salt, or to taste

1/2 teaspoon hot pepper sauce
1/4 teaspoon pepper
1 15 1/2-ounce can dark red kidney
   beans, drained
1 48-ounce can tomato juice
1 14 1/2-ounce can stewed tomatoes
2 cups water
1/2 cup uncooked elbow spaghetti

In a 6- or 8-quart Dutch oven or kettle, brown the ground beef, celery, onion, and garlic. Drain off excess fat. Blend in chili powder, Worcestershire sauce, paprika, salt, hot pepper sauce, and pepper. Stir in kidney beans, tomato juice, stewed tomatoes, and water. Bring to a boil over medium-high heat. Add the uncooked spaghetti. Return to boiling. Reduce heat. Simmer, covered, for 1 hour or until spaghetti is tender. Serve hot with crisp salted crackers or thick slices of homemade bread. Makes about 6 to 8 servings.

Kocsonya (koh-chon-ya)
(Jellied Pigs' Feet)

This is one of my grandmother's basic Hungarian recipes we continue to treasure in our family. What makes it so memorable is the range of texture from chewy to very tender meat suspended in a clear, delicately seasoned jelly. Served with thick slices of fresh homemade bread, it makes a mouthwatering meal that kocsonya connoisseurs rave about. We traditionally serve kocsonya after butchering and for holiday breakfasts. Pigs' feet and pork hocks can be found in or ordered from butcher shops or in major supermarkets.

6 pigs' feet, cleaned, split lengthwise, and cut in two
4 large meaty pork hocks
Cold water
10–12 large firm garlic cloves, or to taste

4–5 tablespoons sweet Hungarian paprika, or to taste
3 teaspoons salt
1 teaspoon pepper

In a large heavy stockpot, combine pigs' feet and pork hocks. Cover with cold water. Cook over medium heat to bring to a slow simmer until a froth forms. Skim off froth and continue to simmer partially covered for 1/2 hour. Add garlic, paprika, salt, and pepper. Add additional water as necessary to maintain a 1- to 2-inch cover over cooking meat. Continue to simmer partially covered for 3 to 3 1/2 hours or until pieces of meat are tender but not falling off the bone.* Place a colander over a large bowl and strain the broth. Season broth to taste. Discard any skin and bones. Distribute the pieces of meat among large containers or mixing bowls. Pour the broth over the meat. Lightly cover and place the filled containers in the refrigerator overnight to jell. Before serving, skim off all fat that has risen to the surface. Serve cold. Makes about 6 to 8 servings.

*Long slow cooking is important to extract the gelatin from the bones and cartilage.

Bohemian Rye Bread

As rye flour is sticky to work with, a sturdy electric mixer with a dough hook is a great help in kneading this fragrant peasant-style bread.

3 cups rye flour
1 cup whole-wheat flour
2 packages active dry yeast
2 cups warm water
1/4 cup dark molasses

1/4 cup butter, melted
3 teaspoons salt
2 tablespoons caraway seeds
3 cups all-purpose flour, divided
Nonstick spray coating

In a small bowl, combine rye flour and whole-wheat flour. Stir to blend. In the large mixing bowl of an electric mixer, combine yeast and water. Stir until dissolved. Add and blend in molasses, butter, salt, and caraway seeds. Add rye flour mixture and beat at medium speed for 2 minutes or until dough is smooth. Cover and let sponge rise until dough is light and doubled, about 45 minutes. Add 1 cup all-purpose flour and beat 1 minute. Stir in enough remaining flour to make a soft dough. Turn out onto lightly floured surface. Knead 8 to 10 minutes or until smooth and satiny. Place in a warm buttered bowl. Turn once to butter top. Cover lightly and let rise in warm place 1 hour or until doubled. Punch dough down. Turn out onto a lightly floured surface and divide in two. Shape each portion into a round loaf. Spray 2 baking sheets with nonstick spray coating. Place loaves on baking sheets. Cover and let rise until doubled, about 40 minutes. Preheat oven to 375°. Slash the loaves with a sharp knife or razor blade. Bake for 30 to 35 minutes or until loaves sound hollow when tapped. Remove from baking sheet onto rack to cool. Makes 2 loaves.

Rich Chocolate Brownies

The texture of these brownies is soft and cakelike, and enhanced by the crunchy walnuts. They are definitely a family favorite thanks to their luscious fudgelike topping.

1 1/4 cups all-purpose flour
1 cup granulated sugar
1 cup packed brown sugar
1/2 cup butter, softened
1/4 cup shortening, softened
1 teaspoon baking powder
1 teaspoon salt

1 teaspoon vanilla
4 large eggs, lightly beaten
3 1-ounce squares unsweetened
    chocolate, melted
3/4 cup chopped walnuts
Chocolate frosting (see recipe below)

Preheat oven to 350°. Grease and flour a 13 x 9 x 2-inch baking pan. In a large mixing bowl, combine flour, granulated sugar, brown sugar, butter, shortening, baking powder, salt, and vanilla. Stir lightly to blend. Fold in eggs and melted chocolate. Beat with an electric mixer on medium speed for 1 minute. Stir in walnuts. Turn into prepared baking pan, leveling surface. Bake for 30 to 35 minutes or until a toothpick inserted in center comes out clean. Remove to a rack and let cool completely. Frost with chocolate icing. Makes about 24 bars.

NOTE: If you desire a thinner brownie, bake in a prepared 15 x 10 x 1-inch baking pan for 25 to 30 minutes.

Chocolate Frosting

3 tablespoons butter
3 tablespoons milk
1 1-ounce square unsweetened chocolate, melted
1/2 teaspoon vanilla
2 1/2 cups powdered sugar

In a small saucepan over low heat, melt butter with milk. Remove from heat. Add premelted chocolate and vanilla. Blend in powdered sugar. Beat until a smooth and fluffy spreading consistency. Spread on cooled brownies. Makes about 2 cups or enough to frost a 13 x 9 x 2-inch baking pan of brownies.

Soft Molasses Cookies

Spicy aromas wafting from the kitchen are a sure sign that molasses cookies are baking. Light molasses has always been a favorite ingredient in baking because it helps keep cookies moist and fresh for many days.

Nonstick spray coating
4 cups all-purpose flour, or more as needed
1 teaspoon baking soda
1 teaspoon salt
1 teaspoon ground ginger
1 teaspoon ground cinnamon
1/2 teaspoon ground cloves or ground allspice

1/2 teaspoon baking powder
1 cup shortening
1 cup sugar
1 egg
1 cup light molasses
5 tablespoons cold coffee or water
1 tablespoon vinegar

Preheat oven to 350°. Lightly spray cookie sheets with nonstick spray coating. In a medium bowl, combine flour, baking soda, salt, ginger, cinnamon, cloves, and baking powder. In a large mixing bowl, combine shortening and sugar. Mix until fluffy. Blend in egg. Stir in molasses, coffee, and vinegar. Mix until well blended. Stir in flour mixture, using more flour if necessary, to make a very soft dough. Drop from a teaspoon 3 inches apart on prepared cookie sheet. Bake for about 12 to 15 minutes or until almost no indentation remains when lightly touched. Let cookies cool for 2 minutes on sheets, then remove to racks to cool completely. Store in tightly covered container. Makes about 3 1/2 dozen cookies.

Variations

Raisin Molasses Cookies: Follow above recipe, but stir in 1 cup raisins after dry ingredients.

Walnut Molasses Cookies: Follow above recipe, but stir in 1 cup finely chopped walnuts after dry ingredients.

The Promise of Seed Catalogs

Recipes in This Chapter

Nothing looks more appealing after a late-January blizzard than a bright gaudy seed catalog tucked in the day's mail. Between its flamboyant pages are promises of extra big or extra small, extra juicy, extra tasty, extra blight-resistant, and even more extra specials for the coming season.

For more years than I care to count, seed catalogs came and went in our country kitchen. Each year it was the same. My mother settled down at the kitchen table to enjoy rosy visions of next summer's flower and vegetable gardens. Right on the cover was a photograph of a bowl of succulent red strawberries. You couldn't miss it. Mother sure didn't.

"Just look at those luscious strawberries," she gushed. "The only thing missing is the shortcake and whipped cream.

"It says here you can order 100 plants that will yield 100 quarts of fruit for just $7.98 post paid. How can you resist that?" She demanded of the room in general.

She waited for Dad to comment, but he never looked up from his *Wisconsin Agriculturist.* When she reminded us how many bowls of strawberry shortcake and ice cream could be made from 100 quarts, she had my attention.

Out of the corner of my eye, I watched her slowly turning the catalog's pages featuring mammoth pumpkins that promised to ripen at 100 pounds in 120 days, 25-pound heads of giant cabbage, and foot-long cucumbers.

Lost in a world of her own, she began to read aloud.

From the sound of her voice, I could tell she'd already planted the radishes, onions, and peas. The lettuce and spinach, carrots and beets, potatoes and beans were next. Any minute she'd start on the tomatoes, cabbage plants, and yellow Hungarian peppers she favored. It happened every winter when Mother was the most susceptible to winter doldrums: Seed catalogs completely mesmerized her into forgetting the snowbanks outside the kitchen doorway, luring her into dreams of a no-work garden and fantastic yields of oversize vegetables.

I understood enough about gardening to know that there were plenty of things those glossy seed catalog pages didn't tell the reader. It never mentioned all the patience it takes to produce the vegetables and flowers in the captivating pictures. It never said anything about the watering and thinning out and more waiting and weeding.

I understood about endless weeding. Ever since I became old enough to understand the simple directions of three beans, four cucumber seeds, and a piece of potato (eye up), Dad encouraged my attention to gardening. It was either that or chores.

So I looked across the room to my father for help. Surely he could call a halt before Mother ordered all eleven varieties of squash, fifteen different bush beans, and more varieties of tomato seeds than we had shelves to hold all the canning jars they'd fill.

My father only smiled his crinkly smile and shook his head. The look in his eye clearly told me you don't think of things like that when studying a seed catalog in the middle of the coldest, nastiest, windy day in January.

Instead, you savor thoughts of fragrant strawberry shortcake and let the butter drip off your chin from the tender cob of steaming corn. It's all possible—the seed catalog promises it.

Leaning over Mother's shoulder, I watched her sigh at each turn of the page from peas to petunias, from great to fantastic.

I slowly began to understand that Mother may be at her most vulnerable and caught in the grip of the promise of the seed catalog, but it is after all her season to dream of her summer garden.

It is all part of the pattern of the seasons—especially the seasons in a country kitchen.

Honey Buttered Parsnips

Mother's garden always included a long row of parsnips. While she harvested other vegetables by late autumn, she mulched the parsnips with a heavy cover of straw and left them in the ground over winter.

"The hard frost gives them a sweet full flavor," she answered our questioning.

We often debated whether the parsnips were the last crop of the previous gardening season or the first crop of the new one. One thing we knew for sure was that once Mother rolled back the parsnip's winter blanket, we were in for a distinctively sweet, earthy treat we all enjoyed. Surely spring was just around the corner.

    4–5 medium parsnips
    Water for cooking
    2 tablespoons butter
    1 tablespoon honey
    1/8 teaspoon nutmeg or cinnamon

Peel parsnips. Cut crosswise into 3/8-inch-thick slices. In a medium saucepan, cook parsnips in a small amount of water for 30 minutes or until tender. Drain. In a medium skillet, melt butter over low heat. Blend in honey and nutmeg. Add parsnips and sauté until glazed, heated through, and delicately browned. Serve warm. Makes about 4 servings.

NOTE: Parsnips can be used in many recipes as a substitute for carrots. You can boil them, roast them, or glaze them. They add a special earthy flavor to soups and stews. Mashed and buttered parsnips also make fine eating.

Scalloped Corn with Cheese

This time-honored dish is easy to make. A prized family favorite, scalloped corn was especially welcome on blustery, snowy days. It's also a great dish to take to church suppers or potluck dinners.

4 slices bacon, chopped
1/2 cup crushed saltine crackers
1 medium onion, chopped
2 tablespoons flour
1 1/4 cups milk
2 eggs, beaten
2 1/2 cups frozen whole kernel corn

1 cup shredded cheddar cheese
1 4-ounce can pimientos, drained
   and chopped
1/4 teaspoon salt
1/8 teaspoon pepper
1/8 teaspoon ground red pepper
Paprika

Preheat oven to 350°. Grease 1 1/2-quart shallow casserole. In a large heavy skillet, cook bacon over medium heat until crisp. Remove bacon and all but 2 tablespoons fat from skillet. Add the cracker crumbs and stir to blend. Set aside for topping. Return remaining drippings to the skillet and cook onion over medium heat until tender. Blend in flour. Gradually add milk and cook, stirring constantly, until thickened. Remove from heat and slowly add eggs, stirring constantly. Blend in corn, cheese, pimientos, and bacon. Season with salt, pepper, and ground red pepper. Pour into prepared casserole. Top with cracker crumbs. Sprinkle with a dash of paprika. Bake for 45 minutes or until nicely browned and bubbly. Serve directly from casserole. Makes about 6 servings.

Harvard Beets

Each year, Mother planted a long row of beets and "put-up" at least 20 to 25 quarts—plenty to brighten our winter meals with their rich, red color. While she served canned beets several different ways, this was her favorite recipe.

1/2 cup sugar
2 tablespoons cornstarch
1/2 teaspoon salt
1/2 cup white vinegar
3 cups cooked diced beets, drained
2 tablespoons butter or margarine

In a medium saucepan over medium heat, combine sugar, cornstarch, and salt. Add vinegar gradually, stirring to blend with sugar mixture. Bring to a boil over medium heat, stirring constantly. Reduce heat and simmer for 2 minutes. Fold in beets. Continue to heat beets in the sauce over low heat, for 15 minutes to absorb flavor. Taste to adjust seasoning, if needed. Add butter just before serving. Makes about 6 servings.

NOTE: No one really knows where the name Harvard beets came from. Some claim that New England cooks have prepared these beets for over 100 years and, since red is the color for Harvard University, the name fits. Others maintain that Harvard University's kitchens hold the honor of first serving this sweet and tangy dish.

Chicken and Rice

By late winter, Mother began butchering some of her older nonlaying hens. This is a delicious way to cook a full grown hen, as slow, long cooking tenderizes the meat. This is a hearty one-dish meal.

1 stewing hen (4 to 5 pounds),
   cut up*
10 cups water, or as needed
1 1/2 cups diced onions
2–3 stalks celery, thinly sliced, leafy
   tops included

2–3 carrots, thinly sliced
1/4 cup snipped parsley, optional
1 1/2 teaspoons salt, or to taste
1/4 teaspoon pepper, or to taste
1 1/2–2 cups long-grain rice**
Paprika for garnish, optional

In a 10- or 12-quart Dutch oven or soup pot, combine chicken and enough water to cover by 2 inches. Bring the mixture to boil over high heat, skimming any foam that rises to the surface. Add onions, celery, carrots, parsley, salt, and pepper. Return to a boil, reduce to a simmer, and cook partially covered for 2 1/2 hours or until chicken is tender. Remove chicken parts from the broth. Take out any bones that may have separated from the meat. Add rice and continue cooking, stirring often, for 15 to 20 minutes or until rice is tender. Trim the meat from the bones and cut into bite-sized pieces. Return the meat to the rice mixture. Mixture will be thick. Taste to adjust seasonings. To serve, ladle into soup bowls. Garnish with a dash of paprika, if desired. Makes about 8 servings.

*If a stewing chicken is not available, you could use a 3- to 4-pound package of chicken parts and adjust cooking time.

**Adjust the amount of uncooked rice to the amount of broth. If you want to serve this dish as a casserole-type main dish as our family did, follow the proportions of 1 cup uncooked rice to 2 cups liquid. The more broth you have, the more uncooked rice to add. If you wish to serve this dish as a soup, decrease the amount of rice accordingly.

Veal Paprika with Noodles

This is a light and utterly delicious Hungarian dish my mother enjoyed serving for both family and special dinners. Its charm is its simplicity.

2 large onions, chopped
3 tablespoons butter or shortening
1 1/2 pounds veal stew or boneless
    shoulder roast, cubed in 1-inch
    pieces
2 tablespoons sweet Hungarian
    paprika

1 teaspoon salt
Water, as needed
1 cup sour cream
Broad noodles, cooked according to
    package directions
Green pepper rings for garnish,
    optional

In a large heavy skillet, sauté onions in butter until transparent. Add veal, paprika, and salt. Brown the meat. Cover skillet and simmer over medium-low heat for 45 to 60 minutes or until meat is tender, stirring occasionally. Add small amounts of water as needed, to prevent over-browning. Slowly fold sour cream into meat mixture 5 minutes before serving. Turn off heat to avoid boiling. To serve, place meat on a warm platter leaving room on one side for the noodles. Pour paprika sauce from the skillet over the meat. Garnish with green pepper rings, if desired. Makes about 6 servings.

Yeast Pan Rolls

Looking back to those long-ago country kitchens, it seemed as if Mother baked either cakes, cookies, pies, or her wonderful yeast breads, and rolls every day. Of course we never complained!

2/3 cup milk	2 packages active dry yeast
2/3 cup sugar	3 beaten eggs
1 teaspoon salt	6 1/2–7 cups all-purpose flour, divided
1/3 cup butter or margarine	1/2 teaspoon nutmeg
2/3 cup warm, not hot, water	Melted butter, as needed

In a small saucepan, heat milk to 115° to 120°. Stir in sugar, salt, and butter. Cool to lukewarm. In a large mixing bowl, add water and sprinkle in yeast. Stir until dissolved. Add lukewarm milk mixture. Add eggs, 3 cups of flour, and nutmeg. Beat until smooth. Add and stir in remaining flour. Turn dough out onto lightly floured board. Knead dough until smooth and elastic, about 10 minutes. Place in greased bowl. Turn once to coat top. Cover and let rise in warm place until doubled, about 1 hour. Meanwhile, grease two cookie sheets. Punch dough down. Turn out onto lightly floured surface. Divide dough in half. Cut each half into 12 equal parts. Using palms of hands, form each part into balls. Place 2 inches apart on prepared cookie sheets. Brush lightly with melted butter. Cover and let rise in a warm place until doubled, about 1 hour. Preheat oven to 400°. Bake rolls for about 15 to 18 minutes or until golden brown. Makes 2 dozen rolls.

Old-Fashioned Burnt Sugar Cake

As far back as I can remember, Mother enjoyed making her special layer cakes. I found this treasured recipe almost hidden on a well-splattered page in her favorite cookbook. I've modified the recipe a bit to include the use of an electric mixer.

1 1/4 cups sugar, divided
1/2 cup water
2 1/2 cups all-purpose flour
4 teaspoons baking powder
1/4 teaspoon salt
1/2 cup butter or margarine
2 egg yolks, lightly beaten

1/3 cup water
1 teaspoon vanilla
2 egg whites
Fluffy caramel frosting (see recipe, page 235)
3/4 cup pecan halves, optional

In a small heavy skillet, add 2/3 cup sugar. Cook over medium heat, stirring constantly with a wooden spoon until sugar is melted and browned. Add the 1/2 cup water and cook for 2 minutes. Set aside and cool. Preheat oven to 350°. Grease and lightly flour bottom of two 9-inch-square cake pans. In a small bowl, combine flour, baking powder, and salt. Set aside. In a large mixer bowl, cream together the rest of the sugar and butter on moderately high speed for 2 minutes. Add the egg yolks, 1/3 cup water, and vanilla. Blend well. Alternately add flour mixture with burnt sugar mixture, beating on low to medium speed after each addition just until combined. Thoroughly wash beaters. In a large mixing bowl, beat egg whites on medium to high speed until stiff peaks form. Gently fold the egg whites into batter just until combined. Pour batter into prepared pans. Bake for 25 to 30 minutes or until a toothpick inserted in center comes out clean. Cool in pans 10 minutes. Remove layers from pans and let cake cool completely. Spread fluffy caramel frosting between layers. Spread top and sides with frosting. Decorate top and sides with pecan halves, if desired. Makes one 2-layer cake.

Fluffy Caramel Frosting

This is a favorite icing for a square cake.

2 egg whites
2 cups packed light brown sugar
1 cup water
1 teaspoon vanilla

In a large mixer bowl, beat egg whites with an electric mixer on medium to high speed until stiff peaks form. In a medium saucepan, combine sugar and water. Cook over medium-high heat, without stirring, until the mixture reaches Hard Ball stage on a candy thermometer. (It should not be so hard that it will become brittle as for taffy.) Pour the hot syrup slowly over the egg whites and beat with an electric mixer on high speed until the mixture is cool and a spreading consistency. Blend in the vanilla. If the icing appears too hard, add a little cold water and continue beating. Makes enough to fill and frost an 8- or 9-inch 2-layer cake or to frost a 10-inch tube cake or a 13 x 9 x 2-inch cake.

Index